"America Can Recover"

Thomas R. Meinders

iUniverse, Inc.
Bloomington

"America Can Recover"

iUniverse books may be ordered through booksellers or by contacting:

iUniverse
1663 Liberty Drive
Bloomington, IN 47403
www.iuniverse.com
1-800-Authors (1-800-288-4677)

Because of the dynamic nature of the Internet, any web addresses or links contained in this book may have changed since publication and may no longer be valid. The views expressed in this work are solely those of the author and do not necessarily reflect the views of the publisher, and the publisher hereby disclaims any responsibility for them.

Any people depicted in stock imagery provided by Thinkstock are models, and such images are being used for illustrative purposes only.

Certain stock imagery © Thinkstock.

ISBN: 978-1-4502-9869-8 (sc)
ISBN: 978-1-4502-9870-4 (dj)
ISBN: 978-1-4502-9871-1 (ebook)

Printed in the United States of America

iUniverse rev. date: 02/23/2011

INTRODUCTION

"America Can Recover" when the representatives of both parties in Washington start to listen to what the people of the United States really want our country to recover from. With the mid-term elections over and the Republicans back in control of the House we will find out if they are going to listen to what the people that elected them are concerned about. Will the Congress start listening to the people of the United States or are we going to get more of the same old corrupt politics?

"America Can Recover" from the past few years of reckless spending programs that the people have not endorsed. Everyone needs to contact their representatives in the Congress and make it known what the American people want. It is not too late if we take actions. Remember if you don't voice your opinions for the changes you feel are correct then you become part of the problem instead of part of the solution. We can accomplish our goal if we set our minds and efforts to the task.

We need to wake up the American voters while we still have some rights in this country. Not only that, we have the God given right to question the actions of the politicians that are making decisions in Washington. We would be fools if we allow ourselves to blindly follow the politicians. We were given brains and were meant to use them to think about the issues that affect our everyday lives in this country.

The uninformed, uneducated and easily manipulated that are among us follow the line of thinking that has been presented to them by the leaders in Washington. It is past time for the citizens of the United States to start realizing what has been happening and make some changes. Fortunately, it is still not too late.

The American voters elected the President and did not look at the facts concerning Obama. The mainstream media tried to make him look like a savior with the hope for change. We have ended up with a President that is in a position that he is not qualified to hold. The President's policies have for the most part been total disasters. The majority of the people are now hoping that the change will come and it better be that this President never gets to run for any office that is in the government.

We need to make sure that everyone that has the right to vote can read English and understand the ballots when they are printed in English. We do not need anymore votes that are decided by the illiterate members of our society because they listened to the propaganda presented by the news media. We do not want any more ballots, government forms, signs, school postings or anything else that is printed in Spanish to appease the illegal population in the United States of America. Stand up for our rights.

The United States needs to develop our own natural resources and reduce our dependence on foreign oil. We need to do this to survive as an independent nation.

Table of Contents

CHAPTER ONE

No Amnesty - Period

I have chosen this to be the first chapter of the book since it will affect the majority of the citizens of the United States. We have about 20 million illegals in the country and we definitely do not need to provide citizenship for these people that have entered our country against the laws of our land. This country needs to look at the quote from the Gettysburg Address: "Government of the people, by the people, for the people, shall not perish from the earth."

With the Republicans taking control of the House and representing a stronger minority in the Senate next year, failure to enact the legislation by year's end dims the prospects for action by Congress to grant a path toward legalization for the nation's millions of undocumented immigrants.

Tamar Jacoby of Immigration Works USA, a pro-immigration employer's coalition, said the defeat won't end Congress' attempts to address the issue but predicted that future legislation will look far different. "Anything that they're going to do is going to disappoint comprehensive immigration reform advocates," Jacoby said. "It's going to be a tough haul" to tackle the subject in the new Congress.

After the House vote, Obama issued a statement pledging to move forward on immigration reform and casting the Dream Act as a way of correcting what he called "one of the most egregious flaws of a badly broken immigration system."

Every American needs to contact their representatives in Congress and make sure that there will not be any legislation that will give amnesty to any illegal. When are the Democrats going to listen to what America wants with regard to amnesty? The Democrats do not listen to anything else for that matter that the people want.

The Democrats face long odds on their immigration measure more commonly known as the "Dream Act".

We Americans hope that the Congress of the United States will not have passed the legislation on the "Dream Act". If it has been passed we need to have it repealed immediately. The citizens of the United States need to make sure that their representatives in Congress understand that the American people do not want any kind of amnesty for any illegal that is in the United States. Every illegal needs to be deported without exception. The Congress needs to step up and face the problems that are being caused by the 20 million illegals that are currently in the United States.

The following article was posted on the Internet by the Associated Press on December 8, 2010.

WASHINGTON – The chance for hundreds of thousands of foreign-born youngsters brought to the country illegally to gain legal status is dwindling as time runs out on the Democratic controlled Congress.

Senate Democratic leaders will try Wednesday to advance legislation that would pave the way for legalizing the young immigrants, over opposition by most Republicans and several in their own party.

The so-called Dream Act is a top priority of Democrats and politically active Hispanic groups, who call it a crucial down payment on a broader immigration overhaul. Critics regard the measure as backdoor amnesty for lawbreakers.

With the GOP taking control of the House and representing a stronger minority in the Senate next year, failure to enact the legislation by year's end would virtually kill the last chance for years for any action by Congress to grant a path toward legalization for the nation's millions of undocumented immigrants.

President Barack Obama's team has made an intense public push for the bill, under pressure from Hispanic activists angry that the White House has not pressed harder for a broad immigration overhaul to give several million illegal immigrants a shot at legal status.

In recent days, the administration dispatched officials from the departments of Defense, Homeland Security and Commerce to argue vociferously in public that the legislation would boost national security and economic growth.

On Wednesday, the White House issued a statement of support for the bill that called the current immigration system "broken."

"While the broader immigration debate continues, the administration urges the Senate to take this important step and pass the Dream Act," the statement said.

Representative Steny Hoyer of Maryland, the Number 2 Democrat, said he expected to bring the measure to the House floor this week, but leaders have held off on scheduling since it is unclear whether it would have the votes to pass.

Obama's drive to enact the legislation and congressional Democrats' determination to vote on it before year's end reflect the party's efforts to satisfy Hispanic groups whose backing has been critical in elections and will be again in 2012.

The legislation would give hundreds of thousands of young illegal immigrants brought to the United States before the age of 16, and who have been here for five years and graduated from high school or gained an equivalency degree, a chance to gain legal status if they joined the military or attended college.

Hispanic activists have described the Dream Act as the least Congress can do on the issue. It targets the most sympathetic of the millions of undocumented people — those brought to the United States as children, who in many cases consider themselves American, speak English and have no ties to or family living in their native countries.

The measure is "very, very far from amnesty," said Cecilia Munoz, Obama's director of intergovernmental affairs, citing the numerous hurdles those eligible would have to scale in order to keep their legal status and eventually become citizens.

Estimates differ widely as to how many young people would be eligible for some sort of legal status under the measure. The Congressional Budget Office has estimated that one version of the bill that applies to immigrants aged 35 and under would let more than 1 million apply for legal status over the next 10 years, and potentially allow 500,000 to receive it.

A newer version of the bill changed to improve its chances only applies to those under 30, which supporters say would limit it to 300,000 or so.

GOP opponents in the Senate circulated a memo calling the measure "mass amnesty," noting that the bill has no cap and no ending date. They contend it could allow even the most dangerous criminals and terrorists to gain legal status.

Now that you have had a chance to read what the Democrats are trying to accomplish I am going to show you what the response of the readers to this article was.

These are uncut and from all over the United States. They should display to the politicians what the citizens of the United States feel about any form of amnesty. They also make statements about securing our borders to stop the flow of the illegals into the United States.

Bring the troops home from Afghanistan and Iraq and it will be far cheaper to feed, arm and direct them on our own borders. They are equipped, trained and able to defend the United States Border and that is what they should be doing. Let the camel jockeys kill each other off and if necessary France, Germany and Italy can finish off the last one standing. This nation is being economically gutted by the illegals in our factories, farms, hospitals, schools and welfare offices. Give them notice unhampered passage home to celebrate their holidays and don't come back. The rest should leave within 60 days or be hunted down and marched across the border. We will take our jobs back--without SEIU, Teamsters, or other union representation. Union workers, you want your jobs back, get rid of the unions that Obama is selling out to.

This Dream Act is not as it appears. Wanting to give legal status to those going to college or serving in the military -- as in the health care plan -- hidden is the statement that these same people can opt out of these requirements. This is strictly for votes and not for the betterment of either the legal who came in and followed the rules or for the American born citizen.

Arizona has the right attitude -- enforce the laws. We can't take care of our own citizens with jobs availability and yet we want to give illegals the right to take what jobs are available from the USA very own citizens.

Don't extend the unemployment benefits free gratis; make them do something for those dollars. There are a lot of streets needing cleaned, debris pick up; volunteering at shelters, etc. Why would anyone actively look for work when they get a pay check to sit at home, not have to worry about clothing, gas, baby sitters, etc? They are further ahead to sit on their butts and let the rest of us take care of them. Granted this isn't all of them.

Stop suing states for enforcing immigration laws; start enforcing laws everywhere. Let those here who want citizenship earn that right; same as anyone else coming into the states. We don't need more welfare and more handouts for the illegals. Making them citizens won't change that problem. Also, when these young people are given citizenship, then their parents, grandparents, aunts, uncles, cousins, etc can come in. Where is this nation's sanity? Forget the votes; work for the people.

How does granting amnesty and citizenship to illegals help increase our national security?

How about finally securing our southern borders and actually enforcing Federal laws already on the books when they're caught? Not much has been done that's effective, even though it's almost 10 years after 9/11/2001.

Won't that dramatically increase national security? Wasn't this also supposed to happen when President Reagan granted amnesty to millions of illegals? All that did was increase the flow of illegals heading north.

Ahhhh the Dream Act, just another piece of legislative toilet paper! I'm sick and tired of Democrats wanting to legalize these dirty rotten illegals. Remember Reagan! It's a slap in the face of every legal immigrant that has ever came to this country, gone thru all the hoops, spent the all the money it takes to become a citizen! How dare they? But remember we voted these idiots into office including Harry Reid, Nancy Pelosi, Kennedy, Dick Derbin, and my own idiot, Michael Bennet.

I don't have a soft spot in my heart for children illegally in the United States. Not when our own children who are citizens may suffer from supporting illegals or 'anchor babies', and not where such humanitarian aid doesn't seem to affect the world view of the United States anyway.

Sounds like the fascist Democrats are trying to break the system even more. If they are illegal they should be deported. No one that came into this country illegally should be allowed to be a citizen. This bill makes a mockery of the law.

I should hope to shout. Illegal is illegal. Try this stunt in any other country in the world and you get put in jail, (and in some you get shot), get deported, etc. Only in America can you come in illegally, live off the backs of working people, get government aid and then demand citizenship. Let's use the last part of the word and "ship" them back where they came from. Let them come in the front door, learn our language and customs, and become legal citizens.

"Hispanic activists have described the Dream Act as the least Congress can do on the issue". That's like salt in my eye. I don't think we owe illegals anything more until we can help our own citizens out of the financial mess were all in.

How is this "Dream Act" to be funded? Also with the unemployment rate so high...are there jobs available for the illegals? Will they be taking legal citizens jobs? One of the major upcoming problems in this country is over population. We should be stopping or at least limiting immigration, at least until we solve our own internal problems. Now before you left wing loonies start saying that if this was the policy when your grandparents entered the country, you wouldn't be here. When our grandparents came to this country, legally I might add, the big bad wealthy business men of the time needed workers to run their factories, there were ample jobs and nobody was coming here to sponge off anybody. Our grandparents came here to work hard and build a new life and become part of a great country. Although they kept their heritage, they become Americans, spoke the English Language and didn't try to change America, for their own special interests. They didn't want hand outs only what they worked for. Think about it.

It seems strange that the American taxpayers pay these senators salary but all they want to do is support the illegals. Time for many of these folks to go home, retire or get beat. It's sad that Reid and Pelosi are still with us since both of them should have been booted.

Has any one of these Senators heard the voice of the people? No, just pandering for the illegal votes. Remember, Reid, it was the Hispanics that put you into office. Another point I must make, you work for the American citizens, We the People do not work for you. There shouldn't be any Dream Act and definitely no amnesty for any illegals.

Any politician who votes for the Dream Act, remember one thing. Americans will vote you out. You are traitors to our country and should be held accountable.

Here's a "Dream Act" for Americans, "Enforce Our Immigration Laws". Our state budgets are suffering in just about every state because the cost of emergency services is out cutting the tax base. Enforce and Deport.

Providing any form of disguised amnesty including "comprehensive", "pay a fine", "Dream Act", is unjust and a slap in the face to deserving applicants from all over the world.

"Comprehensive immigration reform" amnesty would initiate Chain Migration of even more by illegals who often have little desire in assimilation or family planning and potentially erode the culture and sovereignty of this great nation.

Some say "it is impossible to deport 20 million illegals. Actually, the first 50 % would be easy to locate. But, there is an easier way to do it. Fine and jail the landlords and employers that have hired the illegals and provided them a place to live. Terminate all taxpayer funded public services to illegals as allowed by the constitution.

Then the illegals will use the "Feet don't fail me now" program. Self deportation will happen and recent economic history and current events in Arizona have shown "Feet don't fail me now" works. The same way they came here is the same way they can go home. This would provide an effective and taxpayer friendly way for illegals to deport themselves.

Totally agree. As a society, we already recognize that people should not benefit from operating an illegal enterprise (drug dealers). When we catch and convict them, we confiscate all of their assets. Those who employ illegals...and the illegals themselves....are operating illegal enterprises. We should treat them the same way as the drug dealers.

We don't sell American citizenship or pay for you to go to college so you get it for free. If the staffing for the military is needed, re-install the draft and reward our citizens for their service. As for as the Hispanic activists groups is concerned, their interest is not the United States but rewarding people from other nations, expecting us to pay for it, so screw them.

My daughter was not able to get any help for college because she was not: Hispanic, African American, Pregnant, did not have kids, did not live on the streets. She lived at home, worked 35-40 hours a week and went to school full time. She was not able to get any help. But if you are an illegal you get welfare, food stamps and a free education. What happened to those who help themselves gain success? Oh I forgot under our new socialist Democratic government working hard, making money and becoming wealthy is a bad thing to do so the government will take your hard earned money and give to some lazy slob so he can be happy. That is not a great way to treat the people that have worked hard to better themselves.

I'm Latino and I oppose the Dream Act. If passed it will destroy our country and encourage more illegals to stream over the border. I don't feel that it would be fair to reward lawbreakers. I know it's sad that there parents brought them here when they were young but that is not our problem. If anyone is to blame they should blame their parents. We need enforcement of our laws. There should be no double standard. Amen.

If this dream act, or any form of it is passed the "People of the USA" must demand that the President and any member of Congress resign, or be charged with treason. Illegals have spit on our laws and we can't afford this, and no where else in the World is this tolerated. The President and members of Congress need to get this through their thick sculls.

Sneaking into this country = illegal

Having a passport without entry stamp = illegal

Working without a permit = illegal

Knowingly employing an illegal = illegal

Not paying taxes = illegal

Working and using fake ID = illegal + illegal

Working using your legal friend's ID = illegal

Driving with fake or borrowed ID = illegal

Driving with fake ID insurance = illegal

Living 30 to a 1 bedroom apartment = illegal

Reproducing and having a baby on US welfare = illegal

Sending your litter of kids to US schools = illegal

Protesting in the USA = illegal

An act of terrorism = illegal

An act of anarchy against the USA – illegal

If you put this issue to a national referendum...and be diligent in not allowing illegals to vote, as the Democrats have locally made it possible to do in so many places, this idea of fast tracking citizenship would be voted down by the electorate in huge numbers. It would probably be the one, true bipartisan issue since WWII that would be soundly defeated. The Democrats, Republicans, Independents, Blacks, Whites, legal Hispanics, Christians, Muslims, Atheists and Jews would support the legislation. All people who believe in fairness, respect for law, respect for society and culture, respect for doing the right thing, who loudly say no. We have legal ways to enter and stay. To reward people who have come here illegally simply isn't right.

Any of us get caught doing something illegal we get the book thrown at us. Why is it that illegals entering our country get the red carpet treatment? Quit offering illegals a better life. Seal the borders shoot a few trying to swim the big river and that should at least start a word of mouth rumor that the party is over. You can't stop a problem when you keep giving them a good reason to come here illegally!

The Democrats really do not care about the immigrants. They see them as nothing but slam dunk votes and tilting the social scales in their direction of power. They have the black vote by providing social programs but has the black population really done better? The truthful answer is both yes and no. Yes, because they do it themselves and no because they wait on the government. The Democrats will line buses up to get you to the voting booths but not a single bus to get you back across the border. Wake up, the Government is not the answer it is the problem.

Calling an illegal alien an 'undocumented immigrant' is like calling a drug dealer an 'unlicensed pharmacist.'

How about the illegals make an effort to act like they can even follow laws before they demand legal status? They don't seem to understand that by the very fact that they crossed the border illegally that they are criminals. They need to speak English before they demand rights and privileges that are due to citizens. Better yet they need to pack up and leave...and all the liberals who support them need to shut up or leave with them.

I left California for the reason I didn't speak Spanish, in other words I wasn't bi-lingual, and I was born and raised in California. Yes I am white so I moved to Arizona, now this state means business. When has it become okay to deface the American flag like those idiots did and now they want their "Dream Act"? They can do that to our flag and now demand they have rights to be here? I don't think so. One person tried to recover that flag and was stopped by a cop, now where did that cop have the right to stop him? This is outrageous. Shove your dream act where the sun doesn't shine.

The government wouldn't help out with my son's college tuition at all, not one penny. So he is now not going to college but working to save for school. I haven't got much money. I am a white guy born in the United States of America and I have always paid taxes and I have worked my whole life. And I watch as illegal aliens waltz in here to get subsidized by our tax dollars to get a degree. This is just disgusting. What have the liberals done to our country?

This isn't a comment on the "Dream Act", but more a general comment on illegal immigration. I live in South Texas, 10 miles from the border. I can guarantee you that I associate with more illegals in a day than most of you do in a year. I know these people. And for the record, I'm white. These people aren't doctors, engineers, scientists and they certainly don't want to enlist in the military. The jobs they get are fast food workers, janitors, landscapers, construction workers, mechanics and farm workers. If every single illegal was deported tomorrow, the worst that would happen is the price of your head of lettuce would go up by a dollar, or you might have to pay a bit more for your lawn to be fertilized. The idea that illegals are good for our economy is demonstrably wrong. It's been proven that 56% of illegal families are on some form of public assistance. Illegal immigration is wrong, and needs to be stopped NOW.

I am confused. How it is that illegals are allowed to attend our public schools? The public schools financed by our tax dollars. What type of precedent does it set when our government and law enforcement agencies turn a blind eye to the laws of our nation and refuse to enforce them? Perhaps we could all simply find a law we do not care for and openly and defiantly disobey it? Probably not however, but why I am not sure.

The "Dream Act" is a nightmare for the natural born citizens of the United States. Whatever the reform is supposed to mean, what it turns out to be is total amnesty and letting every illegal become legal with a stroke of President Obama's pen. It's wrong, wrong, wrong, and he, along with every single politician who supports it, should be impeached and removed from office and then prosecuted for treason for wanting to give the United States to illegals.

This farce called the "Dream Act" is nothing more than a way for the Democratic Party to manufacture votes for 2012 and future elections. I am truly amazed that they have the gall to cloak it in feigned care for these people, and expect us to take it at face value. If any of you so called politicians do read this, just please, stop this crap. We have had enough.

The only thing that's broken is the bond of loyalty by the White House and the Democratic Party to the country that gave them the best opportunity in the world and to the generations before us who have sacrificed to preserve this.

These "Anti-Patriots" who currently sit in the Senate use their positions as ATMs funded by special interests and have achieved what Stalin, Khrushchev and Gorbachev couldn't do; destroy the backbone of this country.

Now they want to surrender our sovereignty to a foreign power under the guise of "immigration reform". That means putting all of Mexico on America's welfare rolls. Thank the Hispanic congressional caucus. What are you selling next time cancer?

Are we all crazy here, or what? Give the children of illegals a leg up over our own kids to get into college? They will take the place of taxpaying citizens' kids in our state schools, and probably get tuition assistance as well, because they will probably be from low income families. This is truly beyond belief. Harry Reid needs to be horsewhipped. And the media said his opponent, Sharon angle, was crazy?

Fathom the odd hypocrisy that Obama wants every citizen to prove they are insured, but on the other hand, people don't have to prove they are citizens". Now, isn't that something!

Now we got thousands of Americans who fought in the Mexican war that is spinning in their graves at the sheer lunacy of our government and its hidden agenda of merging our country with Mexico. Thanks to our government we are now fast becoming a third world country or banana republic with rampant crime, drugs, low quality of life, near insolvent states, high cost of living, tax dollars going to subsidize immigrants with welfare, health care and a myriad of other problems. Thanks to a government that only cares about perpetuating its own existence

We've seen how these illegal kids think of themselves as being "American" here in Houston. When they protest their status in high schools, they go out and raise the Mexican flag. The idea that they consider themselves anything but Mexican is absurd. How naive do these leftist liberals and Hispanic activists (make that Hispanic nationalists) think we are.

We have neighborhoods and complete subdivisions loaded with weed-growing nose snuffing illegals. They pack three or four families to a house and live like scared gophers. They drive without licenses steal from stores and live like pigs in a barn yard.

I believe that the message is clear from Americans that we will not tolerate any form of amnesty. It will start a real revolt in this country and is not what Americans want. How come the President and Congress can not understand what the citizens America want and act accordingly?

On December 21, 2010 Obama assures Hispanics immigration reform is a top goal of the President

President Obama continues to press for policies that are against what the majority of the citizens of the United States desire. It is all in the hopes of getting more Hispanic votes. The President does not have a clue about the destruction that the 20 million illegals in the United States are causing. President Barack Obama sought to assure Hispanics on that their goal to overhaul U.S. immigration policy would remain a top priority, despite the recent failure of Congress to advance reforms.

The issue is important for many Democrats and could help Obama mend fences with the left wing of his party, which is unhappy at his pact with

Republicans to extend Bush-era tax cuts for richer Americans that he signed last week.

Immigration may also play a role in the 2012 presidential election if Hispanics, an increasingly weighty voter block, blame Republicans for blocking reform. Latinos voted heavily in favor of Obama in 2008.

Senate Republicans on Saturday effectively killed the so-called Dream Act that would have provided a pathway to citizenship for illegal immigrants brought to the United States as children.

Obama immediately voiced deep disappointment over the failure of the Dream Act to advance in Congress, and made plain during an Oval Office meeting with Hispanic congressional lawmakers that he would keep the issue alive.

The President stated that the Immigration reform would remain a top priority for the coming Congress. Obama should start thinking about how to deport the 20 million illegals in the United States instead of working on giving them amnesty and making citizens out of them.

The Republicans will take control of the House of Representatives increase their power in the Senate making hefty gains in the mid term elections. This will make it much harder to advance progressive immigration reform. But Obama says he will keep pushing for the Dream Act and wants a bipartisan approach to its passage. The President needs to stop dreaming since the Americans do not want any form of amnesty.

The American citizens expect the Republicans in the New Year to focus on tougher enforcement of rules to send illegal immigrants back home and to prevent them entering the country in the first place.

CONSTITUTION? WE DON'T NEED NO STINKIN' CONSITITUION!!!

UNFORTUNATELY THAT SEEMS TO BE WHAT MOST OF THE ILLEGALS THAT ARE IN OUR COUNTRY BELIEVE IS THE ACTUAL WAY OF LIFE IN AMERICA.

AMERICA CAN RECOVER WHEN WE WAKE UP AND DEPORT ALL OF THE ILLEGALS AND THEIR FAMILIES THAT ARE IN THE UNITED STATES OF AMERICA!!! THERE CAN NOT BE AND FORM OF AMNESTY FOR ANY OF THE ILLEGALS THAT ARE IN THE UNITED STATES OR COME IN THE FUTURE.

This just might make your day a little brighter!! You, who worry about Democrats versus Republicans--relax, here is our real problem. In a Purdue University classroom, they were discussing the qualifications to be President of the United States. It was pretty simple. The candidate must be a natural born citizen of at least 35 years of age. However, one girl in the class immediately started in on how unfair was the requirement to be a natural born citizen. In short, her opinion was that this requirement prevented many capable individuals from becoming president. The class was taking it in and letting her rant, and not many jaws hit the floor when she wrapped up her argument by stating "What makes a natural born citizen any more qualified to lead this country than one born by C-section?" Yep, these are the same kinds of 18-year-olds that are now voting in our elections!

They breed and they walk Among US...

CHAPTER TWO

The Immigration Problem

The United States is faced with an illegal migrant problem that has grown to unrealistic proportions. Our country does not have the financial resources to support the alleged 20 million illegals that are in the United States. California alone has estimated that there are 10.8 million illegals in their state. No wonder that the state of California is bankrupt. We have been the place every poor and indigent has entered to find the better life. That is commendable, just do it legally? Our borders are not secure and we can watch the news almost daily and see how the illegals are crossing the border carrying backpacks filled with drugs and they are escorted by over the border by armed men. We do not need the illegals or their drugs in the United States and our border security should be one of the most important laws that need to be enforced. How do we get our government to enforce these laws is the question? Absurd isn't it?

The United States has the laws in place but for some reason the Department of Homeland Security does not want to enforce them. Every American needs to send mail and put pressure on them to make sure that they start enforcing the laws instead of suing the State of Arizona. What are they thinking about anyway? Not only does the border need to be secure the United States needs to pass legislation that there is no form of amnesty for any of the illegals or their families. They are criminals by their own actions.

Why is it that the Department of Homeland Security can not understand what the American citizens want? There are about 20 million illegal migrants squatting in tax free America. We can not afford to keep on supporting them. The American people are fed up with the invasion of our sovereign nation by third world outlaws from Mexico and the rest of Central America and South America. We are tired of the refusal of the federal government to secure our borders, opting instead to provide big business with slave labor in the form of illegals from Mexico. This irresponsible policy leaves our nation vulnerable to terrorism and we are totally disgusted with this endangerment of American lives for cheap fruit or vegetables.

The people are disgusted with all the illegals from Mexico who cost the American taxpayers billions of dollars every year in healthcare, education, incarceration and welfare.

The vast majority of the American citizens are in favor of passing legislation like the SB-1070 law that has been passed by the State of Arizona. A survey of the American citizens was taken and the results are as follows:

Immigration Reform ... Should America Follow Arizona's Lead?

The Total Number of people who voted in this poll: 416,455

1) **Should America follow Arizona's lead when it comes to immigration reform?**
   97% voted: Yes

   3% voted: No

   0% voted: Undecided

2) **Do you believe illegal immigrants take jobs U.S. citizens want?**
   85% voted: Yes

   9% voted: No

   5% voted: Undecided

3) **Do you feel being asked for proof of citizenship is a violation of your civil rights?**
   4% voted: Yes

   94% voted: No

   1% voted: Undecided

4) **Would you like to see your state pass a similar immigration law?**
   93% voted: Yes

   3% voted: No

   0% voted: Undecided

   3% voted: I live in Arizona

Our schools have been invaded by non English speaking children from Mexico that are impeding the learning process of students who genuinely belong here and want to have the English language spoken all the time.

The American people are totally disgusted with those who are here illegally and who can not or will not learn to speak English. The taxpayers of the United States are tired of the government wasting millions of dollars each year to print federal documents in Spanish. This is a disgrace to our founding fathers.

The United States needs to stop the illegals that are dumping their medical bills on the backs of the United States taxpayers and then have the audacity to send 20 to 40 billion United States dollars a year back to Mexico. They are not doing anything to help our economy and destroying our employment opportunities in the United States. All of them need to be deported as rapidly as it is possible.

The majority of the crime rate in California is caused by the illegals that are from Mexico. The federal, state and local agencies that refuse to round up and deport the millions of illegals that are destroying the American culture and language. There is no such thing as a Mexican American. If they want to be in the United States they need to want to be an American.

When was the last time you tried to enjoy one of our parks? Try and enjoy a weekend at the park and it will be overrun by illegal Mexican families trashing the place and unsupervised kids running around and blasting mariachi music. Not to mention that no one is speaking English. Call me a racist if you must but I really think that we need to take back American. The vast majority of Americans do not want our country to be turned into a third world country like Mexico.

Americans are totally upset Congress and the President who are trying to convince the people that illegal immigration is good for us and our economy. It does not seem like destroying our economy is good for the United States.

The American taxpayers and voting citizens need to take back America and insist that our representatives in Congress listen to our demands. Some of the things that could be done to alleviate the problem are;

Our economy is the number one issue this election cycle. Secure the border, deport 20,000,000 illegal aliens. The rich would have to pay Americans $1.00 to $5.00 more an hour to hire Americans. Jobs created for Americans. If the rich are not willing to pay Americans that small increase they will find other things to spend their money on. In addition, deporting those 20,000,000 illegals and securing the border would create 10 million jobs. Result, unemployment rate would go down and Americans would once again be able to earn money and spend money. This would be money that is earned in the United States that would be taxed and not sent south to Mexico. The 2008 census report states that nearly 1 in 10 babies born in the USA were to illegal aliens (340,000 babies a year born to illegals). We need to stop the insanity of making all these children automatic citizens. I know it's not their fault but it's just crazy to make every child born to an illegal an American citizen.

There was an article a few weeks ago from the AP stating that 26% of California's population is illegal, 10.8 million illegals. Anyone who's ever lived in California, know there's at least that many there. Our government and both parties have let us down over the last 30 years but Obama's lawsuit against Arizona and all the Democrats standing up and applauding Mexico's president when he denounced Arizona's law takes the cake. It's nothing less than treason.

Over 10 percent of Mexico's population is living illegally in the United States. We've become Mexico's welfare state. It is past time to take America back.

It's easy to dismiss individual programs that benefit non-citizens until they're put together and this picture emerges. Someone did a lot of research to put together all of this data. Often these programs are buried within other programs making them difficult to find. This is a real eye opener as to why the United States of America is Bankrupt.

We need to declare Mexico a failed state and suspend all treaties and other agreements with them. No more taxpayer money to a corrupt government and no more pretending that they are not invading our country.

Obama is at it again. He is trying to shore up the Mexican vote prior to the elections. Obama assured Hispanics that he was not walking away from immigration reform that he promised in his 2008 campaign speeches to overhaul the United States policies. Obama is ramping up his rhetoric against the Republicans to try to persuade the Mexicans that the Democrats are working for the immigration reform and the only reason that it has not been accomplished is that the Republicans are holding everything up. Obama has blamed the Republicans and has urged Hispanics to give the Democratic Party their support. He reaffirmed that they are a very important part and growing voter block.

We are sure that Obama would be against deporting every illegal that is residing in the United States. He does not want the Democratic Party to lose the millions of votes. After all, that is how they are growing their base to try and insure that they are kept in control. President Eisenhower was the last president to deport the illegals and he was one of the most respected presidents in the history of the United States. President Eisenhower presented programs that were for the best interests of the United States. When is Obama going to start backing programs that are for the best interests of the United States citizens? Not the illegal ones that he hopes to turn into Democratic votes by giving them amnesty. America can not let this happen.

In Colorado, 500,000 illegal migrants, plus their 300,000 kids and grand-kids - would move back 'home', mostly to Mexico. That would save

Coloradans an estimated $2 billion (other experts say $7 billion) annually in taxes that pay for schooling, medical, social-services and incarceration costs.

It means 12,000 gang members would vanish out of Denver alone.

Colorado would save more than $20 million in prison costs, and the terror that those 7,300 alien criminals set upon local citizens. Denver Officer Don Young and hundreds of Colorado victims would not have suffered death, accidents, rapes and other crimes by illegals.

Denver Public Schools would not suffer a 67 percent drop-out/flunk-out rate because of thousands of illegal alien students speaking 41 different languages. At least 200,000 vehicles would vanish from our gridlocked cities in Colorado. Denver's 4% unemployment rate would vanish as our working poor would gain jobs at a living wage.

In Chicago, Illinois, 2.1 million illegal migrants would free up hospitals, schools, prisons and highways for a safer, cleaner and more crime-free experience.

If 20 million illegal migrants returned to where they came from, the United States economy would return to the rule of law. Employers would hire legal American citizens at a living wage. Everyone would pay their fair share of taxes because they wouldn't be working off the books. That would result in an additional $401 Billion in IRS income taxes collected annually, and an equal amount for local, state and city coffers. In Florida, 1.5 million illegal migrants would return the Sunshine State back to America, the rule of law, and English.

No more push '1' for Spanish or '2' for English. No more confusion in American schools that now must contend with over 100 languages that degrade the educational system for American kids. Our over-crowded schools would lose more than two million illegal migrant kids at a cost of billions in ESL and free breakfasts and lunches.

We would lose 500,000 illegal criminal migrant inmates at a cost of more than $1.6 billion annually. That includes 15,000 MS-13 gang members who distribute $130 billion in drugs annually would vacate our country.

In cities like Los Angeles, 20,000 members of the "18th Street Gang" would vanish from our nation. No more Mexican forgery gangs for ID theft from Americans! No more foreign rapists and child molesters!

Losing more than 20 million people would clear up our crowded highways and gridlock.

These statistics were from 2007 and they have gotten worse in the last 3 years. America just can not afford to have this kind of strain of our economic system. These statistics are from just a few of the States. Just imagine how serious the problem is when you factor in all of the United States of America?

There is only one thing wrong with sending them all back and that is that Mexico does not want them back.

The immigration problem in the United States has had a development reported on Fox news today. The Homeland Security Department that is headed by Janet Napolitano has an internal memo that is designed to give amnesty to the majority of the illegals in the United States. The memo reportedly will allow this measure to bypass Congressional approval. We can not let this type of policy be enforced in the United States. The majority of the people do not want amnesty of any kind. Why don't the Democrats listen to what the people want?

When will the American people start to look at some of the facts concerning the invasion by 20,000,000 illegals that are destroying the true American way of life? We are going to present some information about what is happening in the United States right now.

How can any branch of the United States government even think about giving this type of person amnesty to become an American citizen? That is absurd.

What most Americans do not realize is that there are several thousand miles of border between the United States and Mexico. This is a vast area that there is not much development around. That alone makes it very difficult to defend and patrol. There should be about 6,000 border patrol agents until the fence is built and over 3,000 of these agents need to be assigned to defend Arizona's borders.

Obama needs to take his family down to the area that has been posted in Arizona. The Bureau of Federal Land Management has responded to the escalating violence by posting signs along a 60 mile highway linking Tucson and Phoenix warning the citizens in English that the area is unsafe because of armed criminals, drugs smugglers and alien smugglers. That is where we want Obama to take his next vacation.

Some things that the United States needs to do that will help solve the illegal problems. They are as follows:

Close every border and access point into the United States of America. Should the Mexican, Canadian, Cuban or any other government be offended by our border policy that is fine? We can live with that much better than we can live with the illegal migrants into the United States.

Locate every illegal person that is in the United States of America and take them back to the closet border where they came from. The simple fact is that they are criminals and illegal and are not deserving of any type of protection by our laws.

This is to include all the anchor babies born in the United States of America during the time that the illegal parents are living in our country.

Current polls show that approximately 75% to 80% of the legal voting American Citizens are in favor of securing our borders. About the same percentages are in favor of adopting laws similar to the Arizona SB-1070.

The government of the United States of America should provide public notice via the mainstream newspapers, the television media and radio in Spanish and English so that everyone that reads or hears will be able to understand. Every illegal in the United States of America has 30 days to get their belongings together and go back over the border that they came from. The illegals that go back voluntarily will not have any record and will be allowed to apply through legal channels to return to the United States.

Every illegal that does not return voluntarily will be hunted down and taken to the border that they crossed into the United States from. A complete record of these illegals will be maintained and they will never be allowed to apply for citizenship in the United States. All of their assets will be confiscated and sold at public auction. That should raise at least $25.00. These types of policy will not only deter any more illegals it will solve the problem of the ones here.

Has anyone heard how the deployment of 1,200 National Guard troops to the area to help monitor the border situation is going? The big problem with that program is that they were only sent there to provide surveillance and support but not to make any arrests. Flying unmanned aircraft over the area is not going to deter anything because the illegals know that they are unarmed. This was just a political ploy by the Obama administration to make the voting citizens think that they were doing something to solve the immigration problem. Again, they are continuing to try to duke the American citizens into believing they are helping. What needed to be done was to deploy 6,000 members of the United States Army, the United States Marine Corps, the United States Navy and the United States Air Force to defend our borders. Then you will see some action and the positive results will follow. The main problem is that it would be successful and that is not what Obama wants. He would rather sue the State of Arizona. The Obama administration would rather give amnesty to the 20,000,000 illegals than have the ACLU and other leftist organizations file complaints against the procedure. The biggest problem is that these organizations think that an illegal has rights. They are criminals and not citizens of the United States. They do not have any rights in the United States because of that fact.

The United States needs to start thinking about our own country and not worry about what other countries are thinking. We are on a destruction course and it needs to be corrected.

CHAPTER THREE

Illegal Immigration Laws of the United States

I am going to provide information about the Immigration laws that are currently in effect in the United States of America. The problem is that our federal government under the leadership of President Obama does not want to enforce these laws. What does America have to do to make the President and Congress take action to insure that the American people are protected from these abuses?

<u>Illegal Immigration is a Crime</u>

Under Title 8 Section 1325 of the U.S. Code, "Improper Entry by Alien," any citizen of any country other than the United States who:

Enters or attempts to enter the United States at any time or place other than as designated by immigration officers; or

Eludes examination or inspection by immigration officers; or

Attempts to enter or obtains entry to the United States by a willfully false or misleading representation or the willful concealment of a material fact; has committed a federal crime.

Violations are punishable by criminal fines and imprisonment for up to six months. Repeat offenses can bring up to two years in prison. Additional civil fines may be imposed at the discretion of immigration judges, but civil fines do not negate the criminal sanctions or nature of the offense.

Each year the Border Patrol is making more than a million apprehensions of people who flagrantly violate our nation's laws by unlawfully crossing United States borders to work and to receive publicly-funded services, often with the aid of fraudulent documents. Such entry is a misdemeanor and, if repeated, becomes punishable as a felony. Over twenty million illegal immigrants live in the United States -- some estimate even more.

In addition to sneaking into the country in violation of the immigration law that requires that aliens be documented for legal entry (referred to as "entry without inspection -- EWI"), others enter with legal documentation and then violate the terms on which they have been admitted by taking jobs that are not authorized or overstaying the authorized period of stay in the country. The INS estimated in 2008 that about 60 percent of the then estimated twenty million illegal immigrants were EWI and 40 percent were over staying their legal requirements. Both types of illegal immigrants are deportable under Immigration and Nationality Act Section 237 (a)(1) (B) which says:

"Any alien who is present in the United States in violation of this Act or any other law of the United States is deportable."

ILLEGAL IMMIGRATION IS NOT A VICTIMLESS CRIME

Apologists for illegal immigration like to paint it as a victimless crime. But in fact, illegal immigration causes substantial harm to American citizens and legal immigrants, particularly those in the most vulnerable sectors of our population--the poor, minorities, and children.

Illegal immigration causes an enormous drain on public funds. The seminal study of the costs of immigration by the National Academy of Sciences found that the taxes paid by immigrants do not cover the cost of services received by them. We cannot provide high quality education, health care, and retirement security for our own people if we continue to bring in endless numbers of poor, unskilled immigrants.

Additionally, job competition by waves of illegal immigrants willing to work at substandard wages and working conditions depresses the wages of American workers, hitting hardest at minority workers and those without high school degrees.

Illegal immigration also contributes to the dramatic population growth overwhelming communities across America crowding school classrooms, consuming already limited affordable housing, and straining precious natural resources like water, energy, and forestland.

BORDER PATROL: NECESSARY BUT NOT SUFFICIENT

The Border Patrol plays a crucial role in combating illegal immigration, but illegal immigration cannot be controlled solely at the border. About half of the illegal alien population is comprised of visa holders that over stay in the United States. These people entered the country legally, but became illegal aliens by their failure to leave the United States upon expiration of their visa. Once entry occurs, there is little chance of detection and virtually no chance of deportation, except for convicted criminals.

WHAT CAN WE DO?

We need a comprehensive program to end illegal immigration; that means ensuring that people who enter illegally or overstay their lawful status will not be able to obtain employment, public assistance benefits, public education, public housing, or any other taxpayer-funded benefit without detection.

The three major components of immigration control deterrence, apprehension and removal need to be strengthened by Congress and the Executive Branch if effective control is ever to be reestablished. Controlling illegal immigration requires a balanced approach with a full range of enforcement improvements that go far beyond the border. These include many procedural reforms, beefed up investigation capacity, asylum reform, improvements in documents, major improvements in INS detention and deportation procedures, limitations on judicial review, improved intelligence capacity, greatly improved state federal cooperation, and added resources.

WHAT ABOUT THE COSTS?

Effective control and management of the laws against illegal immigration require adequate resources. But those costs will be more than offset by savings to states, counties, communities, and school districts across the nation.

Federal Immigration and Nationality Act

Section 8 USC 1324(a)(1)(A)(iv)(b)(iii)

"Any person who . . . encourages or induces an alien to . . . reside . . . knowing or in reckless disregard of the fact that such . . . residence is . . . in violation of law, shall be punished as provided . . . for each alien in respect to whom such a violation occurs . . . fined under title 18 . . . imprisoned not more than 5 years, or both."

Section 274 felonies under the federal Immigration and Nationality Act, INA 274A(a)(1)(A):

A person (including a group of persons, business, organization, or local government) commits a federal felony when she or he: * assists an alien s/he should reasonably know is illegally in the U.S. or who lacks employment authorization, by transporting, sheltering, or assisting him or her to obtain employment, or * encourages that alien to remain in the U.S. by referring him or her to an employer or by acting as employer or agent for an employer in any way, or * knowingly assists illegal aliens due to personal convictions.

Penalties upon conviction include criminal fines, imprisonment, and forfeiture of vehicles and real property used to commit the crime. Anyone employing or contracting with an illegal alien without verifying his or her work authorization status is guilty of a misdemeanor. Aliens and employers violating immigration laws are subject to arrest, detention, and seizure of their vehicles or property. In addition, individuals or entities who engage in racketeering enterprises that commit (or conspire to commit) immigration-related felonies are subject to private civil suits for treble damages and injunctive relief.

Recruitment and Employment of Illegal Aliens

It is unlawful to hire an alien, to recruit an alien, or to refer an alien for a fee, knowing the alien is unauthorized to work in the United States. It is equally unlawful to continue to employ an alien knowing that the alien is unauthorized to work. Employers may give preference in recruitment and hiring to a U.S. citizen over an alien with work authorization only where the U.S. citizen is equally or better qualified. It is unlawful to hire an individual for employment in the United States without complying with employment eligibility verification requirements. Requirements include examination of identity documents and completion of Form I-9 for every employee hired. Employers must retain all I-9s, and, with three days' advance notice, the forms must be made available for inspection. Employment includes any service or labor performed for any type of remuneration within the United States, with the exception of sporadic domestic service by an individual in a private home. Day laborers or other casual workers engaged in any compensated activity (with the above exception) are employees for purposes of immigration law. An employer includes an agent or anyone acting directly or indirectly in the interest of the employer.

For purposes of verification of authorization to work, employer also means an independent contractor, or a contractor other than the person using the alien labor. The use of temporary or short-term contracts cannot be used to circumvent the employment authorization verification requirements. If employment is to be for less than the usual three days allowed for completing the I-9 Form requirement, the form must be completed immediately at the time of hire.

An employer has constructive knowledge that an employee is an illegal unauthorized worker if a reasonable person would infer it from the facts. Constructive knowledge constituting a violation of federal law has been found where (1) the I-9 employment eligibility form has not been properly completed, including supporting documentation, (2) the employer has learned from other individuals, media reports, or any source of information available to the employer that the alien is unauthorized to work, or (3) the employer acts with reckless disregard for the legal consequences of permitting a third party to provide or introduce an illegal alien into the employer's work force. Knowledge cannot be inferred solely on the basis of an individual's accent or foreign appearance.

Actual specific knowledge is not required. For example, a newspaper article stating that ballrooms depend on an illegal alien work force of dance hostesses was held by the courts to be a reasonable ground for suspicion that unlawful conduct had occurred.

IT IS ILLEGAL FOR NONPROFIT OR RELIGIOUS ORGANIZATIONS to knowingly assist an employer to violate employment sanctions, REGARDLESS OF CLAIMS THAT THEIR CONVICTIONS REQUIRE THEM TO ASSIST ALIENS. Harboring or aiding illegal aliens is not protected by the First Amendment. It is a felony to establish a commercial enterprise for the purpose of evading any provision of federal immigration law. Violators may be fined or imprisoned for up to five years.

Encouraging and Harboring Illegal Aliens

It is a violation of law for any person to conceal, harbor, or shield from detection in any place, including any building or means of transportation, any alien who is in the United States in violation of law. HARBORING MEANS ANY CONDUCT THAT TENDS TO SUBSTANTIALLY FACILITATE AN ALIEN TO REMAIN IN THE U.S. ILLEGALLY. The sheltering need not be clandestine, and harboring covers aliens arrested outdoors, as well as in a building. This provision includes harboring an alien who entered the U.S. legally but has since lost his legal status.

An employer can be convicted of the felony of harboring illegal aliens who are his employees if he takes actions in reckless disregard of their illegal status, such as ordering them to obtain false documents, altering records, obstructing INS inspections, or taking other actions that facilitate the alien's illegal employment. Any person who within any 12-month period hires ten or more individuals with actual knowledge that they are illegal aliens or unauthorized workers is guilty of felony harboring. It is also a felony to encourage or induce an alien to come to or reside in the U.S. knowing or recklessly disregarding the fact that the alien's entry or residence is in violation of the law. This crime applies to any person, rather than just employers of illegal aliens. Courts have ruled that "encouraging" includes counseling illegal aliens to continue working in the U.S. or assisting them to complete applications with false statements or obvious errors. The fact that the alien is a refugee fleeing persecution is not a defense to this felony, since U.S. law and the UN Protocol on Refugees both require that a refugee must report to immigration authorities without delay upon entry to the U.S.

The penalty for felony harboring is a fine and imprisonment for up to five years. The penalty for felony alien smuggling is a fine and up to ten years' imprisonment. Where the crime causes serious bodily injury or places the life of any person in jeopardy, the penalty is a fine and up to twenty years' imprisonment. If the criminal smuggling or harboring results in the death of any person, the penalty can include life imprisonment. Convictions for aiding, abetting, or conspiracy to commit alien smuggling or harboring, carry the same penalties. Courts can impose consecutive prison sentences for each alien smuggled or harbored. A court may order a convicted smuggler to pay restitution if the alien smuggled qualifies as a victim under the Victim and Witness Protection Act. Conspiracy to commit crimes of sheltering, harboring, or employing illegal aliens is a separate federal offense punishable by a fine of up to $10,000 or five years' imprisonment.

Enforcement

A person or entity having knowledge of a violation or potential violation of employer sanctions provisions may submit a signed written complaint to the INS office with jurisdiction over the business or residence of the potential violator, whether an employer, employee, or agent. The complaint must include the names and addresses of both the complainant and the violator, and detailed factual allegations, including date, time, and place of the potential violation, and the specific conduct alleged to be a violation of employer sanctions. By regulation, the INS will only investigate third-party complaints that have a reasonable probability of validity. Designated INS officers and employees, and all other officers whose duty it is to enforce criminal laws, may make an arrest for violation of smuggling or harboring illegal aliens.

State and local law enforcement officials have the general power to investigate and arrest violators of federal immigration statutes without prior INS knowledge or approval, as long as they are authorized to do so by state law. There is no extant federal limitation on this authority. The 1996 immigration control legislation passed by Congress was intended to encourage states and local agencies to participate in the process of enforcing federal immigration laws. Immigration officers and local law enforcement officers may detain an individual for a brief warrant less interrogation where circumstances create a reasonable suspicion that the individual is illegally present in the U.S. Specific facts constituting a reasonable suspicion include evasive, nervous, or erratic behavior; dress or speech indicating foreign citizenship; and presence in an area known to contain a concentration of illegal aliens. Hispanic appearance alone is not sufficient. Immigration officers and police must have a valid warrant or valid employer's consent to enter workplaces or residences. Any vehicle used to transport or harbor illegal aliens, or used as a substantial part of an activity that encourages illegal aliens to come to or reside in the U.S. may be seized by an immigration officer and is subject to forfeiture. The forfeiture power covers any conveyances used within the U.S.

RICO -- Citizen Recourse

Private persons and entities may initiate civil suits to obtain injunctions and treble damages against enterprises that conspire to or actually violate federal alien smuggling, harboring, or document fraud statutes, under the Racketeer-Influenced and Corrupt Organizations (RICO). The pattern of racketeering activity is defined as commission of two or more of the listed crimes. A RICO enterprise can be any individual legal entity, or a group of individuals who are not a legal entity but are associated in fact, AND CAN INCLUDE NONPROFIT ASSOCIATIONS.

Tax Crimes

Employers who aid or abet the preparation of false tax returns by failing to pay income or Social Security taxes for illegal alien employees, or who knowingly make payments using false names or Social Security numbers, are subject to IRS criminal and civil sanctions. U.S. nationals who have suffered intentional discrimination because of citizenship or national origin by an employer with more than three employees may file a complaint within 180 days of the discriminatory act with the Special Counsel for Immigration-Related Unfair Employment Practices, U.S. Department of Justice. In additon to the federal statutes summarized, state laws and local ordinances controlling fair labor practices, workers compensation, zoning, safe housing and rental property, nuisance, licensing, street vending, and solicitations by contractors may also apply to activities that involve illegal aliens.

What is the most amazing part of this situation is that these laws have been in effect for 10 to 20 years and there has not been one President or Congress that has done anything to enforce them. It is time to notify each and every member of Congress and make sure that they are going to initiate policies that enforce these laws.

Makes me wonder why the federal government sued the state of Arizona when it is so obvious that they are not doing anything to stop the illegal problem or securing the borders to stop the flow if illegals.

Wake up America it is not too late to correct the illegal problem.

Professor Joseph Olson of Hamline University School of Law in St. Paul, Minnesota, points out some interesting facts concerning the November 2008 Presidential election:

Number of States won by: Obama: 19 McCain: 29

Square miles of land won by: Obama: 580,000 McCain: 2,427,000

Population of counties won by: Obama: 127 million McCain: 143 million

Murder rate per 100,000 residents in counties won by: Obama: 13.2 McCain: 2.1

Professor Olson adds: "In aggregate, the map of the territory McCain won was mostly the land owned by the taxpaying citizens of the country.

Obama territory mostly encompassed those citizens living in low income tenements and living off various forms of government welfare."

Olson believes the United States is now somewhere between the "complacency and apathy" phase of Professor Tyler's definition of democracy, with some forty percent of the nation's population already having reached the "governmental dependency" phase.

If the government grants amnesty and citizenship to twenty million criminal invaders called illegal - and they vote - then we can say goodbye to the United States of America in fewer than five years.

CHAPTER FOUR

Securing Our Borders

Securing the borders of the United States has to be one of the most pressing commitments of the government. But, it has not been and probably will not be for some time. Anyone that is concerned about the illegal entry into the United States needs to contact their representatives and voice your opinion about the lack of security. It will only happen after enough of us write and complain about the lack of protection on our borders.

In August 2010 the government initiated a program to send 1,200 military personnel to the southern border of the United States. Through September 2010 nothing has been heard about the success or failure of this program. From the early reports that were published by the mainstream media these troops were for support and could not arrest anyone that was crossing the border illegally. In addition, reports were that unmanned drone aircraft were flying along the border. The mission was to spot and report to the border patrol. These aircraft were unarmed. Just what was the mission of these troops anyway? They weren't allowed to do anything except call the border patrol.

That is probably why we have not heard anything about what they are doing. Those 1,200 troops are expected to patrol a border that is approximately 1,969 miles long. The illegals just waited for the planes to fly over and then got on their merry way of crossing into the United States. When the war in Iraqi started we heard how it was progressing on a 24 hour basis. We knew where they were bombing, what kind of bomb they were using, how much damage the bombs did and were there any casualties. Why in 2 months does this administration not make any reports as to the success of this troop movement?

My feelings are that this administration does not want to stop the movement of the illegals for some reason. Are we in for another backdoor attempt to grant amnesty to the illegals? The United States could send in real troops that are armed with instructions to apprehend and deport everyone that is attempting to cross the border. The military could use fighter jets to patrol the border and have them armed with live ammunitions so that when they see a crack house or group of illegals crossing they could fire at them. They will more than likely turn back. If not, that is their problem. We need to have results from our government's actions. What good is the Homeland Security when they don't do anything to protect the population of the United States?

The administration should implement a work project similar to the building of the Hoover Dam. There were unemployed workers from all over the United States that went to Nevada and built the dam. If you have ever been to visit the Hoover Dam you realize just how big a project it was. The result was that the government put thousands of men to work and the benefit was that the dam generates the power for the city of Las Vegas, Nevada and sends power to many other areas. It was a major project that put people to work.

The roughly 1,969 miles of border between the United States and Mexico could be a fantastic work project that many thousands of unemployed Americans would volunteer to work on. With the mass work force the project could be finished in a realistic time frame. Instead of paying the workers unemployment benefits the United States would be benefiting from the security of our border. Anyone that is on unemployment that does not want to work on the border will have their benefits stopped unless they are physically unable to do the work. The area where the fence needs to be built is in an area where the work could be done year around. These would be permanent jobs until the fence is completed. Then there will be thousands of jobs that open up due to the lack of illegals that would have flooded the labor market. The training these men received would help them get into construction jobs upon their return to their homes.

The construction of the fence would only allow American workers and not any illegals or green card holders. This is a save America project. The Army Corps of Engineers could be in charge of the project. The labor cost of the fence would be recovered by the decrease in payments to the unemployed and the reduction of natural resources that are being wasted by the government by supporting the illegals.

The problem is that the current administration apparently does not want the border secure for some unknown reason. The United States has the resources to do the job they just need to want to do the job. It is all political and that just is terrible for the American citizens.

What the current administration is neglecting in the process of not securing the borders is that there may be thousands of terrorists that are crossing with the illegals. Not to mention the amount of drugs that is being smuggled across these unprotected borders. Just what is the Department of Homeland Security thinking about? Suing Arizona?

The open space that is created by the oceans and Gulf of Mexico need to be patrolled by military aircraft and the Coast Guard to stop the inflow of illegals from Cuba and Asia to mention a few of the countries that they are coming from.

Things that our government could do with regards to securing the borders of the United States it would go something like the following:

The law abiding citizens of the United States might find it too extreme but the pilots of the Air Force and Navy need to be kept certified. The United States Air Force and The United States Navy have to keep their pilots trained and need to fly a certain number of hours every month to maintain their flight status. Load the planes up with live ammunition and let them use the illegal and drug stations for target practice so the pilots can keep certified. This does not cost the government any more than the regular training missions that need to be flown. It will help solve some of the major problems facing all of the Border States.

The government would be required to support the Border States by providing all the troops that are necessary and support that is required to enforce the immigration laws that are currently in effect. There is not enough time for the politics of the current administration. Quit suing and do the job that is required.

Bring the troops home that were in Iraq and give them a chance to volunteer to protect our borders. They are already trained and have the type of equipment to handle the weather on the border. I would bet that we would have a large number of volunteers trained and ready. Give them the authority to send the illegals back. If they don't want to go inform the illegals that if they don't return we will shoot to kill.

Use all the County Sheriff's that are available along the borders. They know more about what is actually going on then the ICE agents that are not doing their jobs.

Stop wasting the government's resources with all the frivolous lawsuits against the people that are actually protecting our borders.

Build the fence and then patrol it. Build a prison on the border with an open exit leading back to Mexico. Use the illegals to build the prison and wall and do not pay them. Give them a choice, build or go back to Mexico.

I have based these decisions upon reviewing some of the information that has been gathered from news articles written by the media. I have taken information that I collected and tried to explain in a manner that I believe meets my expectations for the United States.

The following information is provided with regard to the wrong Court Ruled on Arizona Law.

In a stunning development that could potentially send the nation into a Constitutional crisis, an astute attorney who is well-versed in Constitutional law states that the ruling against the State of Arizona by Judge Susan Bolton concerning its new immigration law is illegal.

The attorney in question submitted her assertion in a special article in the Canada Free Press. Her argument states in part, "Does anyone read the U.S. Constitution these days? American lawyers don't read it. Federal Judge Susan R. Bolton apparently has never read it. Same goes for our illustrious Attorney General Eric Holder.

But this lawyer has read it and she is going to show you something in Our Constitution which is as plain as the nose on your face.

"Article III, Sec. 2, clause 2 says: "In all Cases affecting Ambassadors, other public Ministers and Consuls, and those in which a State shall be Party, the supreme Court shall have original Jurisdiction. In all the other Cases before mentioned, the supreme Court shall have appellate Jurisdiction."

In other words, the Judge in the Arizona case has absolutely no Constitutional jurisdiction over the matter upon which she ruled. As the Constitution makes abundantly clear, only the U.S. Supreme Court can issue rulings that involve a state. This means that neither Judge Bolton nor the 9th Circuit Court of Appeals in San Francisco, to which the case is being appealed, have any legal standing whatsoever to rule on the issue. Thus, U.S. Attorney-General Eric Holder filed the federal government's lawsuit against the state of Arizona in a court that has no authority to hear the case.

In a related development, another explosive discovery was made by those who actually take the Constitution seriously. The Constitution specifically allows an individual state to wage war against a neighboring country in the event of an invasion, should there be a dangerous delay or inaction on the part of the federal government.

From Article I, Section 10 of the U.S. Constitution, we find these words: No State shall, without the Consent of Congress, engage in War, unless actually invaded, or in such imminent Danger as will not admit of delay."

No one who is actually familiar with the crisis at the southern border can deny that Arizona is endangered by the relentless assault of lawless Mexican invaders who ignore our laws, inundate our schools and medical facilities with unpaid bills, and even endanger the very lives of citizens with criminal drug cartels that engage in kidnapping, murder, human trafficking, and other mayhem, including aiming missile and grenade launchers directly at U.S. border cities from just across the Mexican border. This is every bit as much of an invasion as the nation of Iran sending in a fleet of warships to the Port of Charleston.

The Constitution that forms the basis of the rule of law in this country says that Arizona has legal right to protect itself in the case of inaction or delay on the part of the federal government, including waging war in its self-defense.

This, when coupled with the clear Constitutional mandate that only the Supreme Court hear cases involving the states, should be ample legal basis for attorneys representing Arizona to go after the federal government with a vengeance.

Governor Jan Brewer and the stalwart members of the Arizona legislature have ample legal reason to stand firm against the illegal bullying of an arrogant, lawless federal government. And there are established procedures by which Federal Judge Susan R. Bolton can be removed from her position as a result of her violating her oath of office to uphold and defend the Constitution for the United States of America.

Just weeks after a judge ruled in favor of the Justice Department's challenge to Arizona's immigration law, another showdown between the federal government and the Southwestern state is brewing.

The Department of Justice is threatening to sue Maricopa County Sheriff Joe Arpaio — known among his admirers as "the toughest sheriff in America" and tagged as ruthless and corrupt by his detractors — if he does not cooperate with the feds' year-long civil rights investigation into his police practices.

Arpaio is already the target of another federal inquiry into whether he misappropriated funds and intimidated political opponents, the Washington Post reports. The civil rights department of the Department of Justice, meanwhile, is looking into whether he subjected Hispanics to unlawful search and seizure while conducting crime sweeps in Hispanic neighborhoods. Federal prosecutors are also investigating his "English-only" policy in jails, the Arizona Daily Star reports, which they say may have left Spanish-speaking inmates without access to services.

Arpaio's attorneys told the Post they have been cooperative with the investigation, and contend that the charges against the sheriff are baseless. The ant-illegal-immigration movement in the state has adopted Arpaio as one of its leading spokesmen.

Some Maricopa County officials are worried they may lose millions of dollars in federal funds if the impasse is not resolved.

ICE boasts approximately 19,000 employees in over 400 offices worldwide with an annual budget of more than $5 billion. Last year they deported 340,000 illegal aliens out of 12,000,000 (some say 20, 000,000) which are either 3% or 1.7%. So in an entire year, each employee deported approximately 17 illegal aliens (220 working days per year), or 1 every 2 weeks at a cost of $14,700 per illegal alien. It looks like ICE needs to hire more efficient workers. At this rate, it will take 35 to 60 years to deport just the number of illegal aliens in the country today. Since they are coming in at a rate of about 460,000 a year, ICE gets further behind each year. ICE needs to understand and follow the Arizona sheriff who has individually deported 40,000 illegals. This is just another example of how stupid and incompetent our government is. Send all your ICE agents down to Arizona and learn how to protect our borders.

Sheriff Joe Arpaio is making the Feds look bad, so they are going after him big time. No news there, the Federal Government has to face in the light of it's failures on the Southern Border. By making Sheriff Joe Arpaio out as the villain in this piece they attempt to shift the focus away from those who are really making headway on border security and stopping illegal immigration. How many billions could we save if we had English only language policy in Government as Mexico does with Spanish? Ponder that as you look at the deductions taken out of your paycheck.

Sheriff Arpaoi should be commended for his unwavering stand against illegals coming into Arizona. The federal government needs to discontinue the political actions against the Sheriff. The federal government will not stop at anything to break him. They will go into his income tax returns to see if they charge him with some insignificant thing. If he has received campaign funds the same thing. They will pay county office staff thousands of dollars to get him to unknowingly sign a paper where he authorized the spending of government money on himself. They will try anything and if they can't legally get him with their fraud he may get shot and killed by an illegal or they may just pull an old favorite and kill him in a car accident but they will do their best to put him out of business. It is surprising that they are not shaking down the Governor of Arizona as well.

The Department of Justice goes after a state and then their sheriff that is trying to protect their citizens and does nothing about the patchwork states that are giving out driver license to illegals and cities that are providing sanctuary to illegal criminals that put the nation at risk.

Simply put, if the federal government had enforced the law that were enacted over fifty (50) years ago we wouldn't have this issue today. The only reason it's even in the news as much as it is now, is because Arizona decided to stand up and do something and suddenly they're the bad guy for it. What Arizona needs is support from fellow Americans not to be chastised and then sued by the federal government? A majority of America supports the Arizona law, which is nothing more then a state level version of the federal law. I know the current administration tends to ignore what the majority of the people want.

Here's a question the media never raises: what if Joe Arpaio and Gov. Jan Brewer, and others like them, just reversed their immigration positions? Would Americans shout with glee as millions of Mexicans flooded into the United States? Think about it. Would America be a better place if another 35 or 45 million illegal migrants came flooding into America? Think about life in the big cities if this happened. Who would feed, clothe, educate, and medicate these people? There literally would not be enough people, or resources, to feed all of Mexico. Yet, despite the awareness of these facts, the federal government wants to stop "Sheriff Joe" and others like him, from protecting America. It's not just a border issue it's a country issue.

Tell me why should illegals have any civil rights they are criminals? Go home and get your rights. Has anybody stopped to think about some of the rights that have been taken from these criminal's victims? Lost loved ones that they'll never see again or maybe awakened by a robbery that occurred while they were in there beds sleeping. These victims never asked for it so like Joe has said in the past this isn't the Ritz. If you don't like it don't come back.

That's right federal government, do anything but your job. Arizona is only doing what is right by the law. If the United States government would enforce the laws without having to worry so much about being "politically correct" all the time we would all be a lot better off. As to the speaking English - if you want to be in and live in this country speak the language and quit using the excuse "no speak/no understand" to get off easily. All law enforcement officers should have the guts to stand up and be counted for being against all illegal entries into this country no matter where they are from. Also, if crime is down in Arizona why do you think that is? Arizona crime is down because Sheriff Joe and the Arizona policy of kicking illegals out of this country. That's great, hope he keeps it up and wish all the states and federal government would join in keeping illegals of any nationality out of our country. Use legal means to come in and all are welcome.

When you take up space in America, please come here legally and learn the language. It is English and the easiest language to learn. Then after five years you can apply for citizenship and hopefully you will have learned enough about why you want to live in the United States to pass the citizenship test. If that is too difficult, please go back home. Fly the American flag and be proud to be an American.

The people who cross the border are illegal. They do not respect our laws or our traditions. They want to bring their Mexican heritage (poverty, filth, drugs, illiteracy, crime) to America. They do not want to become Americans. They want to be Mexicans that live off the benefits that Americans provide. We, as a country cannot support this unlimited number of uneducated and unskilled people. It is bankrupting the United States. Just look at California, especially Los Angeles, once a wonderful place to live, work and prosper. Now broke, overrun with illegals that pay no taxes, they live off the freebees furnished by those that obey the law. Even you liberals have to realize when enough is enough. This has nothing to do with race but economics. You liberals, who disagree with me, go down to Los Angeles with an American flag and walk down one of their Mexican streets. You will quickly change your mind and you will see who the racist are.

We need to declare Mexico a failed state and suspend all treaties and other agreements with them. No more taxpayer money to a corrupt government and no more pretending that they are not invading our country.

Securing the borders of the United States is a major problem. We have about 20,000,000 illegals residing in the United States. They did not all come from Mexico or Cuba. They come from all different countries. Unfortunately, we do not have a method of knowing where these illegals came from or whether they are terrorist? What would happen if you crossed some other foreign countries borders?

If you cross the North Korean border illegally, you could get 12 years at hard labor. If you cross the Iranian border illegally, you would be detained indefinitely. If you cross the Afghan border illegally, you would get shot. If you cross the Saudi Arabian border illegally, you will be jailed... If you cross the Chinese border illegally, you may never be heard from again. If you cross the Venezuelan border illegally, you will be branded a spy and your fate will be sealed. If you cross the Cuban border illegally, you could be thrown into a political prison to rot.

If you cross the United States border illegally, You get a job, a driver's license, social security card, welfare, food stamps, credit cards, subsidized rent or a loan to buy a house, free education, free health care, a lobbyist in Washington, A billion dollars worth of public documents printed in your language, the right to carry your country's flag while you protest that you do not get enough respect and in many instances you can vote.

There is something seriously wrong with our system of dealing with the illegals coming into the United States and needs to be corrected now.

We are FED UP with the refusal of the federal government to secure our borders, opting instead to provide big business with slave labor in the form of illegals from Mexico. This irresponsible policy leaves our nation vulnerable to terrorism, and we are FED UP with this endangerment of American lives for cheap fruit.

We are FED UP with people who are here illegally and who can not and/ or will not speak English.

We are FED UP with illegals from Mexico who cost American taxpayers scores of billions of dollars every year in health care, education, incarceration, and welfare.

We are FED UP with taxpayer dollars being wasted to print documents in a foreign language (Spanish).

We are FED UP with illegals who dump their medical bills on the backs of US taxpayers and who still send $20-40 billion a year back to Mexico each year.

We are FED UP with our schools being invaded by non-English speaking children from Mexico who impede the learning process of students who genuinely belong here.

We are FED UP with the fact that federal, state and local penal systems are overrun by illegals from Mexico, again costing US taxpayers billions each year.

We are FED UP with the fact that the overwhelming majority of felony crimes being investigated in Los Angeles have been committed by illegals from Mexico.

We are FED UP with federal, state and local agencies who refuse to round up and deport millions of illegals who are destroying American culture and language.

We are FED UP with politicians, Hispanic and non-Hispanic, who coddle illegals with drivers licenses, lower college tuitions and similar benefits which only encourage more people to invade the US from Mexico.

We are FED UP with the attempted Mexicanization of America.

FED UP Trying to enjoy a weekend at the park (Any Park) and it is overrun by thousands of Illegal Mexican Families trashing the place up with thousands of unsupervised kids running around and blasting Mariachi Music. Not to mention no one speaks English so we (Whites and Blacks) are in the Minority.

Mexico is a third- world slum and we are FED UP with those who want America to be like Mexico.

We are FED UP with corporate lobbyists, Congressmen and our President, etc. who are trying to convince us that illegal immigration is good for us and our economy.

We are FED UP with the illegal aliens who maime, rape, kill, steal from citizens in our homeland! Where do WE go for safety?

Well, it was reported that former Secretary of State Colon Powell continually uses illegals to do work on his home. What a disgrace that is to the American people. The only reason that Colon Powell says that the illegals do essential work in the United States is because he is too damn cheap to hire a legitimate contractor to do the work on his house. It would be great to see the estimates from the real contracting firms that he received bids from. Our guess is that they do not exist.

This article in the Washington Post quotes Powell as urging his party to support illegal immigration because it is "what's keeping this country's lifeblood moving forward" What a stupid statement that is, the reason there is so much unemployment is because of the number of illegals that are in this country doing jobs that people are too cheap to pay American workers to do.

These illegals do not pay any taxes, they do not pay any Social Security, they do not have any Workman's Compensation Insurance and probably drive to his house to do the work with no driver license, no car insurance, and if get hurt either on the way to or at work will have no medical insurance, so we the tax payers are ultimately, thus taking a job away from a legal tax paying American citizen who could use the work, all because Mr. Powell wants to get cheap illegal labor. Mr. Powell should be prosecuted to the fullest extent of the law. Every employee that a contractor or sub-contractor hires has to provide proof that they are eligible to work in the United States. As retired members of the Armed Forces, we are appalled at Colin Powell's total disregard of the law. So there is a black man that believes in slave labor? He is part of the problem...NOT the solution... just like Obama, Reid, Pelosi, and the majority of the Democrats.

In an interview with NBC's Meet the Press Powell said, "a path to legal status should be offered to illegal immigrants because they are doing things we need done in this country." Powell added, "They are all over my house, doing things whenever I call for repairs, and I'm sure you've seen them at your house. We've got to find a way to bring these people out of the darkness and give them some kind of status'" Well, we agree that they need to be brought out of the darkness and give them some kind of status. The status would be criminal and the penalty would be deportation immediately. The United States is suffering from one of the worst periods of unemployment and this bozo wants to use illegals instead of hiring an American contractor.

Of course Colon Powell endorsed Obama for the presidency in 2008. What we are sure of is that Powell only looked at the color of the candidate and did not do any research to find out what he really was.

In lamenting the party's rightward drift Sunday, he said Republicans must not become anti-immigration and spoke in support of legislation that would give certain children of illegal immigrants a way to become citizens if they pursue a college education or military service. Of course he would endorse that program since it would funnel another 800,000 votes into the Democratic Party. Powell's comment that the program is needed to maintain a youthful population in contrast with the aging of Europe and Japan. Does Mr. Powell think that there is not going to be any babies born to real Americans? What a lame duck excuse. We are going to turn the current President into the "DDD President". Check back and we will give you the explanation of DDD. OK?

Powell also said "fringe" elements on the right are taking a low road when they label Obama a foreign-born Muslim and peddle other false theories about non-American influences on the president's character. Obama was born in the U.S. and is Christian. Well, if that statement is true then how come it has been reported that Obama has spent about $950,000 to defend his policy of not having to prove where he was born? In addition, it has been reported that the judge that was handling the cases has since been appointed to the Supreme Court of the United States.

As for attacking Obama on policy and not nonsense is what the Americans are doing. Obama does not have any policies that the majority of the

American citizens are in favor of. When Obama starts presenting programs that the majority of the citizens are in favor of then they will quit attacking him. What Powell does not want to address is the fact that the Obama administration does not present programs that the people want and it is the Democratic Party that is the worst when it comes to trying to discredit the opposition. They never try to explain why the other candidates programs would be worse than there programs.

Powell should be arrested and fined what every other employer of illegal aliens is fined. There's the perfect example of stupidity in our government. How can anyone expect enforcement of our laws when they're being broken at the highest level of government? Will someone explain to us why we need to obey laws of speeding and paying our taxes when this scumbag not only breaks the law, but brags about it as well?

Anyone who hires an illegal is a traitor and should be in prison for doing it, no matter what his or her affiliation. Colon Powell has become a traitor to his country and should be arrested and fined the maximum.

CHAPTER FIVE

What Would America be Like Without Illegals?

If President Obama would currently enforce the laws of the Country and President George W. Bush had honored as well as fulfilled his oath of office on September 12, 2001 after several illegal aliens bombed our country into a national nightmare—If President Bush would have:

- Placed military troops on the Mexican border as well as added 10,000 Border Patrol agents to guard against further lawless crossings.

- Built a double concertino fence along with a 20 foot steel wall that would be finished within two years of September 12, 2001, i.e., it would be in place right now.

- Instructed Border Patrol agents to arrest, prosecute and jail employers of illegal aliens.

- Stopped the massive abuse of Amendment 14 of the US Constitution instead of allow millions of women to cross our borders in order to birth an illegal child on our lands for immediate welfare on American taxpayers' backs.

- Instructed Congress to bring him a bill that stopped massive chain migration of an unending line from the Third World as America is already bursting at the seams with too many people.

- Would have demanded Congress rework the 1965 Immigration Reform Act and made legal immigration a sustainable 100,000 per year with a proviso that every immigrant be fluent in English, be educated, benefit the United States and not come from a terrorist country.

- Stopped 20 million illegal aliens from causing horrific havoc to our schools, medical systems, language, jobs, communities, traffic, gangs, drugs, domestic abuse, rapes, welfare fraud, ID fraud and a host of other calamities now visited upon Americans.

- Stopped four hundred Mexicans peasants from dying in the desert trying to cross illegally into America every year.

Had Bush and Congress done their jobs, we would have a "Day without Illegals." What would that mean to Americans?

- We wouldn't suffer 25 American deaths daily to illegal aliens who kill 13 of us on our own highways and another 12 deaths from gun and knife violence. (Source: Government Accounting Office, 2005)

- We wouldn't have 16,000 new cases of tuberculosis, 7,000 cases of leprosy, countless thousands of cases of hepatitis, Dengue Fever, Chagas Disease, new AIDS cases and thousands of other disease cases thrust upon the American taxpayer. (Source: New York Times, MJ News)

- We wouldn't be paying $1.75 billion annually for anchor babies, and worse, we wouldn't be paying $2.45 billion K-12 annually educating those babies—while our schools devolve into dumb and dumber.

- American workers would be paid American wages at Tyson Chicken, Hormel, Wal-Mart, fast food shops, construction, roofers, landscape and every job Americans have always done for a living wage.

- We wouldn't have 618,000 convicted criminal alien felons in our state and federal prisons at an annual cost of $1.6 billion to us. That's after each of those felon committed a deadly crime on an American citizen.

- We wouldn't have hundreds of thousands of illegals committing car thefts, insurance fraud, driving while drunk and no license, and ID theft.

- We wouldn't have 11,000 MS-13 gang members operating in 33 states as they distribute $100 billion in drugs to our children.

- We wouldn't have $60 billion in cash being transferred out of our country annually.

- We wouldn't have Muslim terrorist cells so easily imbedding themselves into our country for the next attack.

- Our schools could teach our kids in English and not suffer millions of alien kids that cause such consequences as in Denver, Colorado with a 67 percent flunk out/ drop out rate in their high schools.

- We wouldn't have the Mexican flag being marched around our streets as if it's the dominant flag in our country by disloyal and subversive illegal aliens who have no right to be here in the first place.

- Contracting firms and other big employers couldn't cheat, lie, steal and hire illegals for one benefit only: obscene amounts of money.

- Thousands of towns like Hazelton, Pennsylvania with Mayor Lou Barletta wouldn't have to be making laws against illegals to protect his citizens.

- We would enjoy our U.S. Constitution and the rule of law in a pretty darn excellent constitutional republic that is respected and honored by all its legal CITIZENS.

The list accelerates daily. In Denver last week, I.C.E. arrested 122 illegal aliens on a government contracting job. One hundred and twenty-two Americans should have been working those jobs. By mid week, one illegal alien had hung a hangman's noose around a woman and dragged her two miles down the street with his truck until there was nothing left of her to identify her body. That wouldn't have happened if Bush did his job. Not a day later, an illegal alien walked up and shot a man as he pulled his work materials out of his car trunk to start a job. Again, it wouldn't have happened if Congress did its job. I could write another 1,000 incidences each week that occur because illegal aliens run lawlessly around our country with impunity.

What would a day without illegal aliens be like? Would we collapse into an economic heap of misery? Would our country fall to pieces? Would our citizens never get their lettuce picked or their lawns mowed?

As you look at the tip of the iceberg in the aforementioned points, I'd say a day, week, month, year, and in fact, a decade and even a lifetime without illegal aliens would be better than the nightmares they visit upon us every 24 hours.

Have Congress pass legislations so we can find out what it will be like without 20 million illegals.

CHAPTER SIX

America Should Follow Missouri

In 2007, the Missouri General Assembly approved HJR 7 to place on the ballot a proposed constitutional amendment designating English as the official language of Missouri. Voters then went to the polls and approved the measure with nearly 90 percent voting in favor. With that, English became the official language for all governmental proceedings in Missouri. It also means no individual has the right to demand government services in a language other than English. A common language is the cornerstone of a cohesive and united state and country. Ensuring that English is our official language is simply common sense.

Another measure that directly addresses the issue of illegal immigration was passed in 2008. HB 1549 requires our Highway Patrol and other law enforcement officials to verify the immigration status of any person arrested, and inform federal authorities if the person is found to be here illegally. It also allows Missouri law enforcement officers to receive training to enforce federal immigration laws. Furthermore, the bill makes it clear that illegal immigrants will not have access to taxpayer benefits such as food stamps and health care through MO HealthNet. With the passage of this legislation, Missouri sent a clear message that illegal immigrants are not welcome in our state, and that they are certainly not welcome to receive public benefits at the cost of Missouri taxpayers.

2009 saw another significant piece of legislation passed dealing with illegal immigration. HB 390 ensures Missouri's public institutions of higher education do not award financial aid to individuals who are here illegally. The law also requires all postsecondary institutions of higher education to annually certify to the Missouri Department of Higher Education that they have not knowingly awarded financial aid to students who are unlawfully present in the United States. The bill represents another common sense approach to the issue as it ensures taxpayer dollars are not used to subsidize the education of someone who is in our country illegally.

So while Arizona has made national news for its new law, it's important to remember Missouri has been proactive in addressing this growing problem. The laws we have on the books help ensure the rights and benefits of Missourians are preserved for actual Missouri citizens. It's also important to remember that this country has always opened its arms to immigrants, which is why our nation is often referred to as the great melting pot. Immigrants from all parts of the world have helped make our country what it is today. However, our doors are not open to those who try to live in our country illegally. I believe Missouri's laws make that very clear and give our law enforcement officials the authority they need to deal with the problem.

LETTER FROM A RETIRED BORDER PATROL AGENT:

This letter was sent to Tennessee Senator Bill Frist from a retired border patrol agent, and it has more common sense than all the bull being spewed from the Senate, with the exception of a few sensible representatives.

Dear Senator Frist:

There is a huge amount of propaganda and myths circulating about illegal aliens, particularly illegal Mexican, Salvadorian, Guatemalan and Honduran aliens. First, Illegal aliens generally do not want United States citizenship. Americans are very vain thinking that everybody in the world wants to be a United States citizen. Mexicans, and other nationalities want to remain citizens of their home countries while obtaining the benefits offered by the United States such as employment, medical care, instate tuition, government subsidized housing and free education for their offspring. Their main attraction is employment and their loyalty usually remains at home. They want benefits earned and subsidized by middle class Americans. What illegal aliens want are benefits of American residence without paying the price. Second, there are no jobs that Americans won't do. Illegal aliens are doing jobs that Americans can't take and still support their families. Illegal aliens take low wage jobs, live dozens in a single residence home, share expenses and send money to their home country. There are no jobs that Americans won't do for a decent wage. Third, every person who illegally entered this nation left a home. They are not homeless and they are not Americans. Some left jobs in their home countries. They come to send money to their real home as evidenced by the more than $20 billion sent out of the country each year by illegal aliens. These illegal aliens knowingly and willfully entered this nation in violation of the law and therefore assumed the risk of detection and deportation. Those who brought their alien children assumed the responsibility and risk on behalf of their children. Fourth, illegal aliens are not critical to the economy. Illegal aliens constitute less than 5% of the workforce. However, they reduce wages and benefits for lawful United States residents. Fifth, the United States is not an immigrant nation. There are 280 million native born Americans. While it is true that this nation was settled and founded by immigrants (legal immigrants), it is also true that there is not a nation on this planet that was not settled by immigrants at one time or another. Sixth, the United States is welcoming the legal immigrants. Illegal aliens are not immigrants by definition. The United States accepts more lawful immigrants every year than the rest of the world combined. Seventh, there is no such thing as the "Hispanic vote." Hispanics are white, brown, black and every shade in between. Hispanics are Republicans, Democrats, Anarchists, Communists, Marxists and Independents. The so-called "Hispanic vote" is a myth. Pandering to illegal aliens to get the Hispanic vote is a dead end. Eighth, Mexico is not a friend of the United States and hasn't been since 1848.

I think these bleeding heart liberals need to understand that the people (not only Mexicans) that cross the border illegally have broken the law and are therefore criminals. They are not undocumented but illegals. The people of Arizona would like the rest of the country could see how these illegals are destroying our desert, they might support us. If these illegals threw as much trash in your yards, you would want them arrested. I am also sick of hearing people say that we need these people to do the jobs that Americans refuse to do. If they paid a decent wage, Americans would do them. Their next comment is that if the jobs paid more, the cost of the products would go up. What these people don't understand is that it is costing us more money because most of these aliens get subsidized rent, welfare, and it is costing us more in taxes to educate their children.

I wish we could arrest all the politicians that are aiding and abetting the illegal immigrants and who refuse to enforce our laws. Chicago, Denver, Los Angeles and San Francisco, to mention a few, are sanctuaries for illegals and they are there in droves. There are neighborhoods that have but a few English speaking businesses. There have been many arrests of illegals who are gang members and drug dealers. Every politician should be made aware of the Missouri and Arizona laws. They also need to start preparing legislation that will provide the same protections for the entire United States. I hope we do not have to have our representative's press 1 for English. I hope they can read English.

The American Civil Liberties Union is going to fight for the rights of illegal non-citizens. Part of the problem with America is the ACLU. The ACLU is always picking the ludicrous, non-American side of any issue and fighting for it. The ACLU should be deported with the illegals. The Department of Homeland Security and ICE need to do their jobs. Start enforcing the laws of America and start deporting the illegals. How about we quit giving out foreign aid and use that money to deport illegal foreigners from the United States of America?

CHAPTER SEVEN

Eliminate all Earmarks – No Exceptions

Crooked Politics as Usual

Reid and Pelosi are back to their same old politics. The Democrats are trying everything they can to add earmarks to legislation again. The bill to extend the Tax cuts for all Americans has been bombarded with earmarks that are designed to make the legislation more favorable to the Democrats. They know that if they do not add on all the earmarks that they possible can their programs will not get through the Congress in 2011. Cheap politics practiced to the fullest. The earmarks that are being attached to the Tax bill would not stand any chance of passing on their own merit.

The citizens of the United States had better contact each and every representative in your district and make sure that they vote to eliminate all earmarks. If they choose to ignore our requests there is going to be another election in 2012 that we can eliminate another bunch of legislators that are not willing to listen to the people of the United States.

EARMARKS NEED TO BE BANNED

After watching the way government works for the past few days it has become apparent that the policy of earmarks needs to be banned from our government.

We have a country that is in need of programs that will help improve the economy and all the Democrats in the House of Representatives can do is attach earmarks to the bill to extend the tax credits for every American. According to the Democrats we should establish a class system in the United States and penalize the rich for being successful. The Democrats do not seem concerned about what the citizens of the United States have expressed. When will they start to listen to the people? The results of the mid-term elections should have been enough to open their eyes?

The amount of time that the House would have spent on the tax cut legislation could have been reduced to a few hours and the American citizens would be able to relax and know that they will not be hit with an increase in taxes on January 1, 2011.

The problem that the Democrats have is their knowledge that the bills they are trying to attach to the tax legislation would not have a snow balls chance in hell of passing on their own merit.

We could have had the tax situation solved and then passed legislation to extend the unemployment on a separate bill. Both would have been completed in a matter of days. Incidentally, that is what the President and members of the Republican Party had negotiated. Reid and Pelosi have no intention of working with the Republican Party or the President and that is painfully obvious as the days pass.

Legislation needs to be passed in January when the Republicans have control of the House of Representatives. Every bill that is presented must be able to stand on the merits of the bill and be presented to the people of the United States on the Internet for review before the votes are cast. The representatives in both houses of Congress have to start listening to what the American citizens want from their government.

A voting record of how each member of Congress voted on every bill should be made public immediately after the vote. This will be transparency and lead to the representatives voting for what the citizens want.

CHAPTER EIGHT

Unethical Politics

Remember, there are only 545 people making decisions that affect the 308,000,000 American citizens. They are our President, the members of Congress, the members of the House of Representatives and the Supreme Court. We need to make sure that these 545 people understand that they are responsible for making the decisions that protect the welfare of every American citizen. These people determine what the federal budget will be. If they want a deficit, the United States will have a deficit. Hold every representative to the responsibility of creating a balanced budget. When the government wants to solve the illegal migrant problem they have the resources but they need to decide they want to. The stimulus programs were devised by these individuals and did not take into consideration what the citizens wanted. If these 545 representatives that are supposed to be taking care of America would have done their jobs and consulted the American citizen there would not have been 787 billion dollars wasted on the stimulus program. The healthcare fiasco would not have happened if they would have listened to the citizens. Instead, they chose to follow the leader and give in to President Obama. The Constitution which is the supreme law of the land, gives sole responsibility to the House of Representatives for originating and approving appropriations and taxes. Nancy Pelosi is the leader of the majority party and the speaker of the House. She and fellow members, not the President, can approve any budget they want. If the President vetoes it, they can pass it over his veto if they agree to. We need to balance the budget.

The mainstream media operates under a blatant double standard. We watched in 2008 where the media tried to destroy Sarah Palin by digging into everything from the day she was born. Not once did they try and explain the facts about what was accomplished in the State of Alaska while she was Governor.

The mainstream media are always shining intense scrutiny on the Republican candidates. While they turn a blind eye to the history of President Barack Obama's personal history and this was displayed during the 2008 campaign and is still happening. The mainstream media already knows more about the Republican candidate Christine O'Donnell than anybody ever bothered to ask about the president. Obama has yet to release college transcripts and files from his undergraduate work at Occidental College and Columbia University. His college dissertation at Columbia has disappeared. His record at Harvard Law School has disappeared. Many of his official papers during his time as an Illinois state representative have also disappeared. He has never released his full medical records. Where is all the transparency that Obama pledged when he was campaigning for the office of the President of the United States?

During his campaign Obama never referred to his middle name which translates from Arabic to "Good; small handsome one." n English. Now, in 2010, we are seeing the Democrats and the mainstream media putting an all out effort to discredit Christine O'Donnell. They are attacking her from the time she was in high school to everything that was done in her life until today. I for one find it refreshing that someone has the courage to run for one of our highest offices in the country that does not have lots of money. Why are they attacking her because she is not rich and has had to endure life as most of the citizens of the United States? Instead of worrying about how some of the Democratic leaders are going to survive ethics charges they are backing the crocks for re election. Then when they are convicted the Democratic Party can name a replacement of their choosing. Not very democratic but who cares they will retain the seat.

It is disgraceful that the media was learning more about Christine O'Donnell and her college years, her teenage years and her financial dealings than anybody ever bothered to ask about Barack Hussein Obama as a candidate and now as our president.

To compare the biased reporting by the mainstream media we have provided some information concerning the president. You are the thirteenth President under whom I have lived and unlike any of the others, you truly scare me.

You scare me because after months of exposure, I know nothing about you.

You scare me because I do not know how you paid for your expensive Ivy League education and your upscale lifestyle and housing with no visible signs of support.

You scare me because you did not spend the formative years of youth growing up in America and culturally you are not an American.

You scare me because you have never run a company or met a payroll.

You scare me because you have never had military experience, thus don't understand it at its core.

You scare me because you lack humility and 'class', always blaming others.

You scare me because for over half your life you have aligned yourself with radical extremists who hate America and you refuse to publicly denounce these radicals who wish to see America fail.

You scare me because you are a cheerleader for the "blame America" crowd and deliver this message abroad.

You scare me because you want to change America to a European style country where the government sector dominates instead of the private sector.

You scare me because you want to replace our health care system with a government controlled one.

You scare me because you prefer "wind mills" to responsibly capitalizing on our own vast oil, coal and shale reserves.

You scare me because you want to kill the American capitalist goose that lays the golden egg which provides the highest standard of living in the world.

You scare me because you have begun to use "extortion" tactics against certain banks and corporations.

You scare me because your own political party shrinks from challenging you on your wild and irresponsible spending proposals.

You scare me because you will not openly listen to or even consider opposing points of view from intelligent people.

You scare me because you falsely believe that you are both omnipotent and omniscient. (Having unlimited authority and infinite insight)

You scare me because the media gives you a free pass on everything you do.

You scare me because you demonize and want to silence the Limbaugh's, Hannitys, O'Reillys and Becks who offer opposing, conservative points of view.

You scare me because you prefer controlling over governing.

Remember all that is necessary for evil to succeed is that good men do nothing to solve the problems and that is exactly what is happening right now.

Had the voters and the mainstream media investigated this president before the elections we would not have many of the problems that we are facing today. Let's get full disclosure on every candidate before they have a chance to do any damage to the United States. That does make sense, doesn't it?

If there had been a full disclosure on the healthcare bill before it was passed and the people had an opportunity to read the bill before the vote was taken this bill would never have been passed. Both houses of the Congress were controlled by a majority and the vote was crammed down the throats of the people. When President Obama was campaigning he was stating how everything would be transparent and the people would have a chance to read the documents. This is the prime example of corrupt and unethical politics.

Then this corruption continued right up to the elections in November 2010. The Democrats tried to sneak a bill through that would repeal the "Don't Ask and Don't Tell" bill that would have had a major impact on the military of the United States while we were at war. They wanted to slip this through before the elections instead of waiting for the study that was being conducted to see how it would affect the military and what the ramifications might be. The other unethical part of this was they were also attaching a bill that was called the Dream Act. The Dream Act would have paved the way for amnesty to about 800,000 illegal Mexicans that are living in the United States illegally. Thank God for the Republicans and the fact that they were able to defeat this legislation. The Democrats wanted this so that it would appease the Hispanic community and try to capture a larger vote for the Democratic candidates in the election.

The American people do not want amnesty for the illegal migrants that are living in the United States. Then we have the president's aunt that is living in government housing that is costing $850.00 per month and she is also getting $700.00 per month subsistence allowance. Then the president's aunt has the audacity to go on record that she should be made a United States citizen. The only thing that this woman should receive is a one way ticket to Kenya with instructions never to return to the United States. One wonders just how much political pressure has been used by the president to allow his aunt to stay in the United States. Oh, that's right, she has been granted asylum due to the fact that she might be in danger because of her relationship to the president. Why then are all the other relatives living in Kenya not living in danger? Next will the president be moving all his relatives to the United States? Another thing, why hasn't the president been caring for his aunt instead of her being a leach on the government? He is rich enough to afford helping her.

Well, Senator Reid is up the underhanded policies that are the trend with the Obama administration. The Democrats are trying to pass legislation to repeal the "Don't Ask and Don't Tell" bill and attach Reid's "Dream Act" as an ad on to the original bill. This and all future administrations need to understand that every bill that is presented by either the Congress or the House of Representatives needs to be for the benefit of all the citizens and be able to stand alone so that the passage will be on the merits of the individual bill. The policy of attaching legislation that everyone knows will not pass to a bill has to be stopped.

The repeal of the "Don't Ask and Don't Tell" bill is opposed by every commanding general in all four branches of the military. They want to have studies about how it is going to affect the military prior to trying to repealing the bill. What harm can it do to find out whether it is a good for the military or not? The Obama lemmings want to make sure the repeal is passed while it controls the Congress and House of Representatives. That way they can appease the Hispanics at the same time. The underhanded policies are what are making so much dissatisfaction among the voting public.

The administration is fully aware that the stand alone "Dream Act" would not have a snowballs chance in hell of passing on the merit of the bill. This is just more sleazy politics in an attempt to try and shore up more votes from the Hispanic community.

The Republican Party needs to band together and support every politician that is running on their ticket. The candidates that have lost in the primaries need to stop feeling sorry for themselves and back the winner. These career politicians that have lost to the up and coming movement stop whining and congratulate the winners and support them. It has been quite obvious that the voting people of your jurisdictions wanted someone that presents change and new ideas.

After the November elections it would be a good time for all the members of Congress, the House of Representatives, the President, the Vice President, the heads of the Justice Departments and every other department head that is appointed by the President will be required to show absolute proof that they are American Citizens. This will be in the form of a certified copy of the birth certificate from the hospital where they were born. In addition, all the above mentioned officers will provide proof of their educational and military background. No exceptions.

Congress hasn't sent the president any of the 12 annual spending bills it must consider to pay for government programs when the new budget year starts on Oct. 1. With lawmakers leery of voting for spending increases, prospects for much action on these bills are slim. Congress instead will have to vote to keep agencies funded at current levels to avoid a shutdown.

Among others on the may-not-happen list are a bill to authorize defense programs for 2011 and a bill requiring greater disclosure of corporate and union spending on campaign ads.

Senate Republicans have balked at the defense bill because the House added a provision to repeal the don't ask-don't tell policy for gays serving in the military. GOP aides said it would require three weeks or four weeks of debate time if that provision remains.

The campaign spending bill is in response to a Supreme Court ruling lifting restrictions on election ad spending. Advocates of the measure, which requires greater identification of those financing ads, had hoped it could be passed before the November elections. But in July, the Senate fell three votes short of overcoming a GOP filibuster. Naturally, the Democrats blamed the Republicans for doing nothing. Maybe it was just a bad bill.

Also on tap, to the dismay of Democrats, are House ethics committee trials of two prominent Democrats, Reps. Charles Rangel of New York and Maxine Waters of California, for alleged ethics violations. One or both of those trials could begin before the fall election. These two are both too busy trying to get re-elected. The audacity knowing that they will more than likely be convicted of ethics violations and kicked out of Congress.

The Senate planned to open a trial on the impeachment of U.S. District Court Judge G. Thomas Porteous Jr. The House in March approved four impeachment articles charging the Louisiana judge with taking payoffs and lying under oath. Who said being a judge made you honest?

It's the first impeachment trial since the one held for former President Bill Clinton in 1999. The Senate acquitted Clinton. If Porteous is found guilty, he would become the eighth federal judge in U.S. history to be impeached and convicted.

The House could take up a $4.5 billion Senate-passed child nutrition bill, promoted by first lady Michelle Obama that would create healthier standards for food served in schools. They want more watermelon served in schools everywhere. You don't have to tell me that is a racist remark it was nor intended to be.

The Senate could act on a rules change, pushed by some of its newer members, to end the custom where a single senator can secretly block a bill or a nomination. Sure they do then no one will be able to block legislation that they do not want.

CHAPTER NINE

Repealing Legislation

There are some critical pieces of legislation that have been passed since President Obama was elected. It just seems like every piece of legislation that Obama signs into law are against what the people are against. Obama did not learn anything from his failed stimulus program that spending money will not create jobs.

On September 26, 2010 President Obama signed into law H. R. 5297 the Small Business Bill. This bill authorizes $30 billion for new loans and $12 billion in tax relief programs for small businesses. Over the next 10 years the American citizens can expect this bill to cost about $300 billion to the American taxpayers. In his signing speech President Obama stated. "It was critical that we cut taxes and make more loans available to entrepreneurs." Obama is presenting this program in the hopes that it will encourage more votes for the Democratic Party in the mid-term elections.

At the signing Obama estimated that the new bill would create 500,000 new jobs from the $42 billion bill. When will someone please teach Obama some simple math? If it costs $42 billion to create those jobs it means that the taxpayer is going to be spending $84,000 per new job. Is it any wonder that the people do not have any confidence in the President? There are many great programs that can be implemented that will create jobs as a much lower cost to the taxpayer.

No where does this bill suggest how it is going to be paid for. Obama is just trying to secure a few more votes by this legislation. The banks that are being provided the additional $30 billion to provide small business loans and they will probably impose strict lending policies on the small businesses and charge them excessive loan processing fees just like they did with the $787 billion stimulus bill. The only people that really benefited were the banks that controlled the money. The mortgage refinancing program was a total failure due to the fact that the rate of interest on the mortgages did not come down far enough to off set the cost of refinancing. The mortgage refinancing program was a great deal for the banks that lower the interest rate which will be long term income to fees that are short term income to shore up their balance sheets and profitability. The program was just another scam presented by Obama to try and secure more votes by making the people that needed the help the most were misled into thinking that they would be able to recover from their mortgage problems.

What President Obama is not recognizing is the fact the small businesses are not going to borrow money to create new jobs. The jobs will be created when the businesses can afford to hire the employees and those employees will be producing enough product or services to justify hiring them. No one in business believes the President's policy of spend, spend, spend and borrow to pay for it. It is just very bad economics. Businesses are worried about how many extra expenses they are going to incur by the costs of the new government spending bills. The healthcare bill has a new requirement that is going to require all businesses to prepare 1099"s for any transaction over $600.00. All that is going to accomplish is adding expenses to the small business and the preparation of these forms will more than likely be ignored by most small businesses.

This is nothing but a junior version of the highly unpopular Wall Street bank bailout. It needs to be repealed as quickly as possible. The government just can not afford to take on another $42 billion in debt next year with possibility of that figure increasing to $300 billion over the next ten years. Where are the politicians that understand we need to stop the spending spree that we are on? President Obama needs to start looking at what the people want instead of what he wants. This is just another of the President's very stupid plans and it will not work anymore than the $787 stimulus bill. America needs to wake up so that we can recover America.

Health Care Bill – H.R. 4872 – Reconciliation Act of 2010 needs to be repealed. This bill was pushed by the Obama administration for about a year at the expense of every thing else until the Democratic members finally convinced a couple of Independents to vote for it. No one knows for sure what is in the H.R. 4872 bill or had an opportunity to find out before it was voted on and signed into law by Obama. This bill is expected to add over $900 billion to the deficit. We are predicting that in the initial year of the bill it is going to add $300 billion to the deficit this year. That is not what the American people want. Not to mention that majority of the people tried to get the administration not to pass the legislation.

On the day the legislation was signed into law by President Obama "This is a somber day for the American people," said Representative John A. Boehner, the House Republican leader. "By signing this bill, President Obama is abandoning our founding principle that government governs best when it governs closest to the people."

The Attorney General of more than twenty states has filed lawsuits against the Department of Justice contending that the healthcare bill is unconstitutional.

We are not against healthcare. We are against passing a bill that does not allow enough time for the members of Congress to read the bill and debate some of the provisions of the bill. There have been attachments to the bill that are absolutely insane. An example is the provision that small businesses are required to prepare a 1099 form for any transaction that exceeds $600.00 and forwarded them to the Internal Revenue Service. Who really knows just how many pork projects have been attached to this bill.

The only way this is going to be repealed is for everyone to contact their respective representatives and let them know that you do not want the bill in the present stage. We were promised transparency by the President and this bill was just the opposite. It was crammed down the throat of the Americans without anyone of the members of Congress having time to read the bill. There was no transparency or respect for what the people wanted. This was old Chicago politics like never before witnessed in the federal government. It has to stop and when it does we will have a better chance of recovering America from the politicians.

The balance of the $787 billion stimulus bill that has not been expended needs to be repealed. The program has not worked and any further funding would just be a further waste of government spending that is contributing to the deficit.

If we can get our representatives to cancel these three bills that were all passed without the approval of the majority of the people of the United States we can reduce the deficit by about $700 billion. Repealing these programs would be a good start to solving the problem of the continued federal deficit.

Here is another example the H.R. 2454 the Cap-and-Trade anti-global warming energy reform bill and the promise of President Obama and Democratic congressional leaders that they would conduct legislation in public. In reality, they are writing and moving the bill forward behind closed doors in the Senate. It was reported that the Senators sponsoring the bill would not introduce the bill via the normal Senate process. They are planning on introducing the bill by handing it over to Senate Majority Leader Harry Reid, D-NV.

This will bring back memories of "If we introduce it, it'll get referred to committees," Lieberman said, it is reported that Samuelson said, "We want him to be able to work with it and bring it out onto the floor as a leader whenever he's ready." This procedure would leave Reid free to present the bill to the Senate for a vote whenever he thinks it will have a chance to pass or attach the bill to another piece of legislation that has a chance to pass and be signed into law. Once more the President is promoting politics without any sign of transparency to the public.

The Senate previously submitted the Kerry-Graham-Lieberman compromise version of a bill similar failed to get any where in the Senate in spite of the vigorous efforts of Obama and Boxer, D-CA.

These bills would establish an artificial government controlled market that would buy and sell credits that are designed to lower emissions. They would promote the lowering of carbon emissions caused by the use of fossil fuels like our standard oil, coal and natural gas.

Of course when you eliminate the majority of the fuels that have been used for centuries that leaves the wind, thermo and solar all of which are underdeveloped and not cost efficient.

I might be confused but it seems to be a pattern of behind the back Chicago style politics being implemented at the highest level of government.

This is another case of behind closed doors politics as we already witnessed with the Obamacare, stimulus, small business bill and many others. The President campaigned on transparency and the government of the United States needs to start informing the public before any more legislation is passed by the Congress and signed into law by the President.

There are persistent articles that have been written about how this will affect the future of some very prominent Democrats that are both in office and have left office. Well get into the details further when the situation develops. One thing is for sure, the American public is going to absolutely stunned and sickened.

Does any one else remember a quote from the Speaker of the House promising the American people that "The most honest, most open and most ethical Congress in history." What seems to be lost in her philosophy are the facts. The House of Representatives has two members that are currently being charged with ethics violations and facing trials.

The biggest step that needs to taken for the country to recover is to eliminate all the crooked politicians. That means we will have to check out the candidates.

There is another bill that the House Democrats will be trying to approve. House leaders also appeared unlikely to call a vote on a Senate passed school nutrition bill favored by first lady Michelle Obama. The bill is opposed by liberals because it would cut food stamp benefits to find the money to pay for better school lunches. The Senate passed the $4.5 billion legislation in August. This is just what the United States doesn't need to have. The president has been able to force enough legislation down our throats we do not need his wife to start spending more of the government money. In this case it is just rob Peter to pay Paul.

CHAPTER TEN

The 2011 Federal Budget

Table S-3 Baseline Projections of Current Policy (In Billions)			
Receipts	2010	2011	2012
Individual income taxes	951	1,126	1,271
Corporate income taxes	176	293	333
Social Insurance and Retirement Receipts			
Social Security payroll taxes	635	674	720
Medicare payroll taxes	180	192	208
Unemployment insurance	51	60	66
Other retirement	9	8	9
Excise taxes	74	80	83
Estate and gift taxes	17	24	21

Customs duties	24	29	33
Deposits of earnings -			
Federal Reserve	77	79	67
Other miscellaneous	18	18	18
Total Receipts	2,213	2,583	2,829
Proposed Deficit	1,430	1,145	934
Proposed Expenditures	3,643	3,728	3,762

This information is reported in the proposed budget for the year ending September 30, 2011. These are the latest budget figures that are available. The figures are taken from page 149 of the proposed budget that was submitted by President Obama. I know some of the columns do not add up but that is how they are reported in the budget. What's a billion here and there?

What President Obama has submitted in his budget proposal is continued increases in spending and no way of paying for what programs are being passed into legislation. This type of activity is going to ruin this great nation. We need to stop the spending and increase the corporate income tax structure in the United States. I am going to show just how unfair the tax structure is for the individual income tax payer in the United States. We do not need to raise the corporate income tax rate. What we need to do is make sure that the corporations are paying income taxes on the earnings that they are reporting to their shareholders. I am going to prepare a brief listing of major corporations in the United States and see if their earnings were taxed at 35% what the income taxes should have been. We can tell by the above projections what the government is expecting to receive in corporate income taxes. This list is only the tip of the iceberg.

The earnings that are shown are taken from the stock quotes posted on December 7, 2010. They were not picked for any particular reason except that they reported on the quote system that they had earnings reported during their latest fiscal year in excess of one billion dollars.

I wonder how many of these companies actually paid income taxes on the earnings that were reported on the quote system to justify the price of the shares. I do not know but was just asking the question.

Corporation	Symbol	(LFY) Earnings
Abbott Labs	ABT	$5.75 B
American Express	AXP	$2.13 B
Baxter International, Inc.	BAX	$2.20 B
Becton Dickinson & Co	BDX	$1.32 B
Boeing Co.	BA	$1.31 B
Bristol Myers Squibb Co.	BMY	$10.61 B
Chevron Corp.	CVX	$10.48 B
Colgate Palmolive Co.	CL	$2.29 B
Conoco Phillips	COP	$4.86 B
CSX Corp.	CSX	$1.15 B
Deere & Co.	DE	$1.86 B
Dell, Inc.	DELL	$1.43 B
Deutsch Bank	DB	$6.94 B
Duke Energy	DUK	$1.08 B
Dupont	DD	$1.76 B
Ebay, Inc.	EBAY	$2.39 B
Emerson Electric Co.	EMR	$2.16 B
Exxon Mobile	XOM	$19.28 B
Federal Express	FDX	$1.18 B
First Energy Corp.	FE	$1.01 B
General Dynamics Corp.	GD	$2.39 B
General Electric Co.	GE	$11.00 B
General Mills, Inc.	GIS	$1.53 B
Goldman Sachs Group, Inc.	GS	$13.38 B
Halliburton Co.	HAL	$1.14 B
Hewlett Packard Co.	HPQ	$8.76 B
Home Depot, inc.	HD	$2.66 B
Honeywell Int'l, Inc.	HON	$2.15 B

Humana, Inc.	HUM	$1.04 B
Intel, Inc.	INTC	$4.37 B
IBM	IBM	$13.42 B
Johnson & Johnson	JNJ	$12.27 B
J. P. Morgan Chase	JPM	$11.73 B
Kellogg Co.	K	$1.21 B
Kimberly Clark Corp.	KMB	$1.88 B
Lockheed Martin Corp.	LMT	$3.02 B
Merck & Co.	MRK	$12.86 B
Morgan Stanley	MS	$1.36 B
McDonald's Corp.	MCD	$4.55 B
McKesson Corp.	MCK	$1.26 B
Microsoft Corp.	MSFT	$18.76 B
Monsanto Co.	MON	$1.11 B
Norfolk Southern Corp.	NSC	$1.03 B
Northrop Grumman Corp.	NOC	$1.69 B
Oracle Corp.	ORCC	$6.14 B
Raytheon Co.	RTN	$1.94 B
Roche Holding Ltd.	RHHBY	$7.20 B
Southern Company	SO	$1.71 B
Texas Instruments, Inc.	TXN	$1.47 B
U S Bancorp	USB	$2.20 B
Union Pacific Corp.	UNP	$1.90 B
Verizon Communications, Inc.	VZ	$3.65 B
Walgreen Co.	WAG	$2.09 B
Wal-Mart Stores, Inc.	WMT	$14.34 B
Wells Fargo & Co.	WFC	$12.28 B
Total Reported Earnings		$270.68 B

I am sure that there are many more companies that reported earnings during their last fiscal year. These were just randomly selected. Assuming that these 55 companies paid the average rate of 35% income tax they would have paid $94.73 billion in taxes to the federal government.

Considering that the federal budget expects to receive a total of $293 billion during the tax year ending September 30, 2011. It means that the remaining corporations in the United States are only going to contribute $198.27 billion to the government. That does not seem like a fair distribution considering that there are about 30,000 publicly traded corporations in the United States and there are no records available concerning the number of private corporations.

The Congress needs to enact legislation that will close the loop holes in the income tax codes. Every corporation in America that has operations in foreign countries must be forced to pay income taxes to the United States for all income earned in another country. In addition, corporations that have out sourced the jobs from America to foreign countries must be required to pay an excise tax on the out sourced salaries. The excise tax would be equal to 100% of the amount of wages that are out sourced to another country. This will allow for more employment of the American workers that are currently unemployed. The excise tax would be used to replenish the unemployment funds.

This example illustrates how the federal government thinks solving the budget short comings can be resolved. How the politicians in Washington are actually taking care of our country. The following is an example of what the politicians think a haircut is;

One day a florist went to a barber for a haircut. After the cut, he asked about his bill, and the barber replied, 'I cannot accept money from you; I'm doing community service this week.' The florist was pleased and left the shop. When the barber went to open his shop the next morning, there was a 'thank you' card and a dozen roses waiting for him at his door.

Later, a cop comes in for a haircut, and when he tries to pay his bill, the barber again replied, 'I cannot accept money from you; I'm doing community service this week.' The cop was happy and left the shop. The next morning when the barber went to open up, there were a 'thank you' card and a dozen donuts waiting for him at his door?

Then a Congressman came in for a haircut, and when he went to pay his bill, the barber again replied, 'I can not accept money from you. I'm doing community service this week.' The Congressman was very happy and left the shop. The next morning, when the barber went to open up, there were a dozen Congressmen lined up waiting for a free haircut.

And that, my friends, illustrates the fundamental difference between the citizens of our country and the politicians who run it. Both the politicians and diapers need to be changed often and for the same reason.

CHAPTER ELEVEN

The Return of Industry

The United States is rapidly becoming the very first post industrial nation on the globe. All great economic empires eventually become fat and lazy and squander the great wealth that their forefathers have left them, but the pace at which America is accomplishing this is absolutely amazing. It was America that was at the forefront of the industrial revolution. It was America that showed the world how to mass produce everything from automobiles to televisions to airplanes. It was the great American manufacturing base that crushed Germany and Japan in World War II. But now we are witnessing the deindustrialization of America. Tens of thousands of factories have left the United States in the past decade alone. Millions upon millions of manufacturing jobs have been lost in the same time period. The United States has become a nation that consumes everything in sight and yet produces increasingly little. Do you know what our biggest export is today? Waste paper! Yes, trash is the number one thing that we ship out to the rest of the world as we voraciously blow our money on whatever the rest of the world wants to sell to us. The United States has become bloated and spoiled and our economy is now just a shadow of what it once was. Once upon a time America could literally out produce the rest of the world combined. Today that is no longer true, but Americans sure do consume more than anyone else in the world. If the deindustrialization of America continues at this current pace, what possible kind of a future are we going to be leaving to our children?

Any great nation throughout history has been great at making things. So if the United States continues to allow its manufacturing base to erode at a staggering pace how in the world can the United States continue to consider itself to be a great nation? We have created the biggest debt bubble in the history of the world in an effort to maintain a very high standard of living, but the current state of affairs is not anywhere close to sustainable. Every single month America goes into more debt and every single month America gets poorer. So what happens when the debt bubble pops?

The deindustrialization of the United States should be a top concern for every man, woman and child in the country. But sadly, most Americans do not have any idea what is going on around them. For people like that, take this article and print it out and hand it to them. Perhaps what they will read below will shock them badly enough to awaken them from their slumber. The following are 19 facts about the deindustrialization of America that will blow your mind....

#1 The United States has lost approximately 42,400 factories since 2001. About 75 percent of those factories employed over 500 people when they were still in operation.

#2 Dell Inc., one of America's largest manufacturers of computers, has announced plans to dramatically expand its operations in China with an investment of over $100 billion over the next decade.

#3 Dell has announced that it will be closing its last large United States manufacturing facility in Winston-Salem, North Carolina in November 2010. Approximately 900 jobs will be lost.

#4 In 2008, 1.2 billion cell phones were sold worldwide. So how many of them were manufactured inside the United States? Zero none nada.

#5 According to a new study conducted by the Economic Policy Institute, if the United States trade deficit with China continues to increase at its current rate, the United States economy will lose over half a million jobs this year alone.

#6 At the the of July 2010, the United States trade deficit with China had risen 18 percent compared to the same time period a year ago.

#7 The United States has lost a total of about 5.5 million manufacturing jobs since October 2000.

#8 According to Tax Notes, between 1999 and 2008 employment at the foreign affiliates of United States parent companies increased an astounding 30 percent to 10.1 million. During that exact same time period, United States employment at American multinational corporations declined 8 percent to 21.1 million.

#9 In 1959, manufacturing represented 28 percent of United States economic output. In 2008, it represented 11.5 percent.

#10 Ford Motor Company recently announced the closure of a factory that produces the Ford Ranger in St. Paul, Minnesota. Approximately 750 good paying middle class jobs are going to be lost because making Ford Rangers in Minnesota does not fit in with Ford's new "global" manufacturing strategy.

#11 As of the end of 2009, less than 12 million Americans worked in manufacturing. The last time less than 12 million Americans were employed in manufacturing was in 1941.

#12 In the United States today, consumption accounts for 70 percent of GDP. Of this 70 percent, over half is spent on services.

#13 The United States has lost a whopping 32 percent of its manufacturing jobs since the year 2000.

#14 In 2001, the United States ranked fourth in the world in per capita broadband Internet use. Today it ranks 15th.

#15 The rate of manufacturing employment in the U.S. computer industry is actually lower in 2010 than it was in 1975.

#16 Printed circuit boards are used in tens of thousands of different products. Asia now produces 84 percent of them worldwide.

#17 The United States spends approximately $3.90 on Chinese goods for every $1 that the Chinese spend on goods from the United States.

#18 One prominent economist is projecting that the Chinese economy will be three times larger than the U.S. economy by the year 2040.

#19 The U.S. Census Bureau says that 43.6 million Americans are now living in poverty and according to them that is the highest number of poor Americans in the 51 years that records have been kept.

So how many tens of thousands more factories do we need to lose before we do something about it?

How many millions more Americans are going to become unemployed before we all admit that we have a very, very serious problem on our hands?

How many more trillions of dollars are going to leave the country before we realize that we are losing wealth at a pace that is killing our economy?

How many once great manufacturing cities are going to become rotting war zones like Detroit before we understand that we are committing national economic suicide?

The deindustrialization of America is a national crisis. It needs to be treated like one.

America is in deep, deep trouble folks. It is time to wake up

It is only a matter of time until our currency will be totally worthless. Unless your stocks are in international companies, they will be devalued also. The price of commodities, precious metals, industrial metals, copper, tin, aluminum, etc., will continue to increase with the price of energy and food. Once the collapse begins, if anarchy doesn't rule, it will take ten years or more to begin to dig out of the mess and try to rebuild America. Will you have the resources to weather the drought period? There could be untold riches awaiting those who prepare now. But it takes money to make money. Be sure you are holding something of value when the dollar takes a nose dive. And pray we are able to maintain a first class military. We will need it when China and Russia combine to form the largest and most modernized military ever imagined. In twenty years China will be able to outspend us three to one on military expenditures. I am sure they wish us the best of health.

CHAPTER TWELVE

Confidence in America

One of the road signs in the state of Washington showed a grinning Obama holding a sign that said; "Transparency means… in secret, behind closed doors! The President vowed to suspend all federal funding to the state of Washington until this and others like it are removed. Wouldn't have been better if the President started to provide the citizens of the United States the transparency that he promised during his campaign speeches? Due to copyright laws I was not able to include the actual photo. If you would like a copy emailed to you it can be requested at meinders@aol.com

Here are some of the famous quotes that our federal government has spoken publicly. It really makes you wonder just about the intelligence level of our politicians.

With statements like these we can understand just why there isn't a high level of confidence in our representatives in Washington, D.C.

The federal government is now petitioning to have these signs removed or Washington State will be denied additional monies for interstate high ways? Washington replied they will succeed from the Union rather than be intimidated by President Obama.

Great Orators

"One man with courage makes a majority." - Andrew Jackson

"The only thing we have to fear is fear itself." -Franklin D. Roosevelt

"The buck stops here." - Harry S. Truman

"Ask not what your country can do for you; ask what you can do for your country." - John F. Kennedy

Then there are today's genius quotes.

"It depends what your definition of 'Sex' is?" -Bill Clinton

"Those rumors are false ... I believe in the sanctity of marriage." - John Edwards

"I invented the Internet." - Al Gore

"America is ... is no longer, uh, what it ... it, uh, could be, uh, what it was once was ... uh, and I say to myself, 'uh, I don't want that future, uh, uh for my children." - Barack Obama

"I have campaigned in all 57 states." - Barack Obama Quoted 2008

"You don't need God anymore, you have us Democrats." - Nancy Pelosi (Quoted 2006)

"Paying taxes is voluntary." - Senator Harry Reid

"Bill is the greatest husband and father I know. No one is more faithful, true, and honest than he." - Hillary Clinton (Quoted 1998)

And the most recent gem of wisdom from the "Mother Moron"

"We just have to pass the Healthcare Bill to see what's in it." Nancy Pelosi (Quoted March, 2010)

We are really lucky to have such brilliant minds in charge of what once the greatest country in the world.

Then we have President Obama making comments that our economy is on the right track despite job losses. The President said that economic trends were favorable even after the job report was released and the latest unemployment data still showed that 9.8% of Americans are unemployed.

As usual the President attacked the Republican policies which he said were hampering his capacity to ease the unemployment. When is our President going to wake up and realize that the Democrats have been in control of both houses of Congress since January 2007? Does our President ever accept any blame for his failed economic and unemployment policies? All I can remember this President doing is present spending bills that do not have any way of being paid except by increasing the deficit.

The president chose to highlight the fact that the economy had now produced "nine straight months of private sector jobs growth" but admitted "that news is tempered by net job losses."

Here we go again "The Republican position doesn't make much sense, especially since the weakness in public sector employment is a drag on the private sector as well," Obama said. "The trend line in private sector jobs growth is moving in the right direction," Wow, if our economy and unemployment are moving in the right direction we are in for a world of trouble for the next two years.

Only in the world of Obama could a loss of 95,000 jobs translate into "jobs growth not being fast enough" You actually have to be growing jobs for growth to 'not be fast enough. No one has "hampered" Obama's plans to ease the unemployment crisis except Obama. He's going about it the wrong way and has no qualifications or expertise in this area. His advisors are jumping ship because even they are making bad decisions. Obama can't go a day without blaming someone else for his woes, mostly he blames the other party when no on else comes to mind. If economic trends are "favorable" in Obama's words, why is he thinking of another stimulus? Any private sector growths are not due to anything Obama has done, it is due to the ingenuity of the private sector, not the government.

I think that everyone should make it their business to check the backgrounds of all the people who are in the White House, including all of those Czars's Obama has appointed. Obama did say to judge him by the people he surrounds himself with. He keeps saying that we are going in the right direction, that means a government take over, to bring America down, Remember Spread the Wealth? The truth is he does not care about your jobs, your health care, just his idea of the New World Order. I would doubt that anyone in the country voted for that.

What is really annoying the citizens of the United States is that in the face of continued economic bad news, Obama trots out the same old broken record: This is Bush's fault, it would have been worse without our policies and voters need to give us still more time.

Then we have Greenspan declaring that fear and confidence is undermining the United States recovery.

A crisis of confidence grips the economy, Greenspan says. That helps to explain why GDP growth slipped to 1.7 percent in the second quarter from 3.6 percent in the first quarter. The capital investment should have climbed sharply in recent months since corporate profits have been increasing rapidly. The fact that the investments have fallen short combined with a collapse of the consumer sector has depressed the economy and severely ruined the confidence for a recovery.

That combined with the government's failed economic recovery through the $787 billion stimulus added fuel to the lack of confidence by the American citizen.

The uncertainty of the housing markets and the problems with the foreclosures and the documents related to them are going to create a severe lack of confidence for years. Until the legality of the foreclosure documents and how they are going to affect the homeowners will put a severe handicap on the real estate markets and further destroying the confidence of the average American.

Why didn't the current group of Democrats learn anything from one of their previous presidents about the economy? John F. Kennedy, a Democrat, cut taxes. Why? Because he knew that by cutting taxes business would improve, more people would be working, and more money would flow into the federal treasury. Kennedy would look at the current crop of Democrats running things from Washington and throw up. Cutting taxes will stimulate the economy far more than bail outs and all of that other stimulus programs that Obama and his comrades in Congress have forced on us. The problem though is this. Additional income to the treasury comes in and then Congress spends like a drunken sailor on shore leave. Spend less than you make and you won't go broke. It is not the federal government's job to take care of everyone and it is not given the power to do so by the Constitution. All of these entitlement programs that Congress has cooked up as a means to get votes from their constituents will lead us to ruin. We must stop the spending on programs that do not have any means of providing the funds to pay for them.

Within a few months after the Republicans take control of both houses of Congress the country will see the economy take a major step towards recovery. The tax cuts and more importantly the cutting of the spending will give business entrepreneurs the confidence to get back into the market place and therefore creating more jobs. Even the biggest fool knows that you can't create jobs by spending and more spending without any reasonable method of paying for it.

There is no way that our country will return to America the Beautiful until the government stops trying to create a third world country within our borders.

Americans will have more confidence in our government when it starts to follow the Constitution of the United States of America. "Government of the people, by the people, for the people, shall not perish from the earth."

CHAPTER THIRTEEN

Poverty in America

The American voters need to be made aware of the problems that we are facing. The following information underscores the need for the United States to have a change in the direction that our government is headed. The stimulus hasn't been successful, the economy is in dire straights, immigration is causing major problems, healthcare programs need to be repealed and we need to stop providing funding for programs that primarily help the unions.

The poverty level in the United States is on track to post a record for the largest gain in the year 2009. The number of people in the United States who are living in poverty is on track for a record increase on President Barack Obama's watch, with the ranks of working-age poor approaching 1960s levels that led to the national war on poverty.

The latest census figures for 2009 to be released soon will indicate that the recession ravaged first year of the Democrat's presidency will show grim statistics for the year.

These figures are going to be unfortunate for President Obama and the Democratic Party weeks before the important elections when control of Congress is at stake.

The report is expected to show that the anticipated poverty rate increase will be anywhere from **13.2% to 15%** and would be another blow to Democrats struggling to persuade voters to keep them in power.

In order to keep the poverty level from growing the administration must implement important anti-poverty efforts. The efforts need to be to keep the economy growing and making sure there are enough jobs being created in the private sector. The president has stressed the government's commitment to helping the poor achieve middle class status. Again the president is stressing the formation of a class structure within the citizenry of the United States. That seems to be in conflict with the principals that the United States was founded on. We need to grow the economy faster and create more jobs in the private sector instead of the government and then the poverty level will have a chance of improving for everyone. Unfortunately, the government is not doing anything to create jobs or improve the business atmosphere currently in the country.

The bad news is that not everyone is in agreement with the president and there are some demographers who closely track poverty trends found wide consensus that 2009 figures are likely to show a significant rate increase to the range of 14.7 percent to 15 percent.

These estimates would indicate that some 45,000,000 people in the United States were poor last year. That would be an astounding 1 in 7 people in the United States were poor last year. It would be the highest increase in any single year since the government began calculating poverty figures in 1959. The previous high was in 1980 when the rate jumped 1.3 percentage points to 13 percent during the energy crisis.

The demographics of this crisis in the United States will show that among the 18 to 64 year old working population we can expect the rise in the poverty level to be beyond the 12.4% and that would be up from 11.7% from the previous year. There was another Democratic president, Lyndon B. Johnson that launched a war on poverty that expanded the federal government's role in social welfare programs from the education to the health care sectors. This country does not need any more educational or health care sectors created to help solve the problem. We have too many of those already. What we need is a public works program similar to the construction of the Hoover Dam during President Hoover's administration. That put people back to work and helped solve the poverty problems.

Other statistics are more than likely to show the following:

- The number of children living in poverty will increased from 19 percent to more than 20 percent.

- The number of Blacks and Latinos were disproportionately hit, based on their higher rates of unemployment.

- That the metropolitan areas that posted the largest gains in poverty included these cities; Modesto, California; Detroit; Michigan; Cape Coral and Fort Myers, Florida; Los Angeles, California and Las Vegas Nevada.

Well, it looks like the president will have to start playing the blame card again. There is no way that he will accept any responsibility for these increases even though they are reporting for the year 2009 during which he was president. These figures will not be surprising to most of the working group of citizens that have been on unemployment of having to work part time jobs. It is doubtful that it will encourage any new programs from the administration to help solve the problem. The president should not blame anyone else for the desperate circumstances of desperate people. That would be wrong in my opinion. But that's not to say it won't happen.

When the results are completed the Republicans in the midst of an increasingly strong drive to win control of the House, if not the Senate, would get one more argument to make against Democrats in the campaign homestretch.

Democrats almost certainly will argue that they shouldn't be blamed. They're likely to counter that the economic woes and the poverty increase began under President George W. Bush with the near collapse of the financial industry in late 2008. Even though that is not true the Democratic theory will sway the voters that are already leaning toward the Republicans and Independents in the public opinion polls as the terrible news keeps piling up on the Democratic Party.

The news on poverty will more than likely lead to a large number of Hispanics and blacks that are traditionally solid Democratic constituencies could be inclined to stay home in November if, as expected, the Census Bureau reports that many more of them were poor last year. This will worry the Democrats even more since they traditionally have had a very large percentage of their votes coming from these two sections of the population.

The bad news for the citizens is that these findings will more than likely put pressure on Obama to expand government safety net programs ahead of his re-election bid in 2012 as the Republicans and Independents heap more criticism about the federal spending and annual deficits. These are major areas of concern for independent voters whose support is critical in every election. Unfortunately, we do not need any more government programs. We need to stop the spending and eliminate government programs.

This current recession has the potential to push the poverty level for the working age Americans to a level that could reach a 50 year peak. It is past the time for the people to demand a renewed program to attack the problem of increased poverty in the United States. We need to force our government into taking positive action and create programs to help the improvised citizens of our country.

The key factor to remember is as long as the unemployment level in the United Sates remains in the 10% range the number of American's that are living in the poverty level will continue to grow. When the unemployment level goes back to the level of 4.8% that it was when the president took office the poverty level in the United States will decrease. The more Americans are working the better the whole economy will be and these jobs need to be created now.

The poverty level in 2008 stood at $22,025 for a family of four that is based on official government calculations. The calculation is based on cash income before income tax deductions and includes capital gains which are very unlikely for the people living at the poverty level. It does not factor in non cash items such as tax credits, food stamps or the stimulus programs sponsored by the government.

If you thought the poverty level was bad at 15% wait until the beginning of next year when the government plans to publish new supplemental poverty figures that are predicted to show much higher numbers then we have ever known. The new figures will take into consideration the rising costs of medical care, transportation and child care. This change is expected to add to the ranks of the poverty level by including seniors who are drawing social security. Of course the president could reinstate the automatic raises to the recipients of social security. Every little bit will help the seniors.

The Census Bureau reported that the poverty in rate in the United States has jumped to 14.3% which is the highest rate since 1965. This report was posted by KCCI channel 8 in Des Moines, Iowa on September 16, 2010.

The poverty rate increased from a 13.2% poverty level in 2008 and is expected to be another blow to the Democrats that are struggling to persuade voters to keep them in power. After reading this article we decided to do some research and see what states have the highest unemployment rates, which states have the highest poverty rates, which states have the highest populations and which state they voted for in 2008. The Census Bureau reported that about 43.6 million people were in the poverty level last year. That meant that 1 in 7 working age poor were in poverty last year.

The highest unemployment rates in the United States were in California, Nevada, Oregon, Illinois, Indiana, Ohio, Michigan, North Carolina, South Carolina, Florida, Mississippi and Rhode Island. These facts can be verified by the Bureau of Labor Statistics of the United States Department of Labor.

An interesting statistic is that during the 2008 Presidential elections the following states voted Democratic: California, Nevada, Oregon, Illinois, Indiana, Ohio, Michigan, North Carolina, Florida, Mississippi and Rhode Island. There were other states that voted Democratic. It should also be noted that the states that voted Republican were in the states with the lowest unemployment rates. Could there be any connection to the unemployed and people in the poverty class voting Democrat instead of thinking about who they vote for?

How is Obama going to blame Bush for this? It was the results of Obama's first full year as President. Things are not getting any better. A report came out today that foreclosures were up 25% on the year in the United States. This after massive foreclosures in 2008 and the rate is up 25% this year. The banks took back over 95,000 properties during the month of August which was a 3% increase from July.

In excess of 2.3 million homes have been repossessed since the start of Obama's administration. Does anyone recall that President Bush tried to stop the lending policies that were irresponsible? President Bush on 17 different occasions tried to rein in the Democrats on the lending policies that were started by President Carter and given steroids by President Clinton. Their policies were that every American needed to own their own home. It started policies that led to no down payments, no credit checks and no verification of income.

One sure way we can decrease the poverty level in the United States would be to make sure that the borders are secure and then deport every illegal that is taking jobs and services from the government and the people. There must not be any amnesty for any illegal in the United States. Yesterday, Senator Reid (D- NV) was making statements that we should allow the illegals to spend 2 years in college or serve in the military. What kind of an idiot would even suggest this policy? Who is going to pay for the college education and why would anyone want an illegal to serve in the United States military? They would want a legal holiday on May 5th and salute the Mexican flag.

The amazing thing is how the Associated Press reported the unemployment claims downturn they made sure to point out in the headline that it is the lowest level in 2 months. They still are not reporting the fact that foreclosures are the highest since the housing crisis began. All of that is news today, and they are clearly reporting with bias!

Part of the unemployment problem in Nevada is caused by Senator Reid and President Obama. They are the ones that pushed for the cancellation of funding for the Yucca Mountain Project for our nuclear waste. The Yucca Mountain Project is funded through taxes on utility bills of citizens from over 30 states. Yet, Obama and Reid cancelled the funding for the project and are forcing the closure of the project. This will cost the citizens of Nevada thousands of jobs and will incur billions of dollars in litigation costs to the tax payer.

Keep this in mind. The elite Bankers have posted record breaking profits this year. The elite corporations have posted record breaking profits this year. The government has given these groups tax breaks money and jobs as well as contracts. We have not been provided with the full extent of the money provided to the Corporations. That is because our government does not have the transparency they were promised by Obama during his election speeches. The bankers got somewhere around $1.7 trillion give or take a few billion. Think about it. Who is pulling the strings of America? It is not the citizens like the Constitution mandates. It is not too difficult to realize that the government does not work for the citizens of the United States. Remember that 7 of 10 of the richest congressmen are Democrats. We need to have the courage to take this country back from the greedy politicians that have used the race card and are trying to create a class welfare system for their own gain.

What do you think would happen to the number of Americans living in the poverty level if we did not have 15 to 20 million illegals living in the United States? The numbers would change for the better and we would also decrease the amount of crime in the United States.

CHAPTER FOURTEEN

The Recession

The good news for the people is that the recession has officially ended according to the government. Now if you believe that there is a great bridge for sale in southern South Dakota. Doesn't go anywhere but the price is right and it will continue to increase in value every year.

WASHINGTON (Reuters) – The recession ended in June 2009, making it the longest downturn since World War Two, the National Bureau of Economic Research said on Monday.

The NBER, considered the arbiter of U.S. recessions, said it chose that month based on examination of data including gross domestic product, employment and personal income.

This has to be the worst and most hollow story that we have ever read on Yahoo! News. How do they define 'recession? What is our normal unemployment rate and how do today's numbers compare to that average? How much debt have we accumulated in the last year? What are the housing values and the number in foreclosure? These are all important questions not even mentioned in the article. Show us the metrics.

What is amazing is that Yahoo News would even report such drivel. This appears to be another attempt by the Obama administration to blow smoke up the citizens again to try and gain a few votes. Anyone with an ounce of common sense knows that the recession is not over and more than likely has turned into a very serious depression. The Obama administration has been operating under the false assumption that if you tell a lie often enough that the people will believe it.

The mainstream media has to be kidding. Some of the more obvious statistics reveal that the recession has not ended. Consider the fact that unemployment is being reported by the administration and the mainstream media at 9.8%. The real number when you consider all the facts would be in the range of 16% to 20%.

The value of most homes in America has decreased in some areas by over 50%. There have been about 8 million jobs lost and the economy is not creating enough jobs to even keep up with the population demand which is about 400,000 new jobs per month. The Obama administration has not presented any programs that will provide incentives for companies to increase manufacturing and produce "Made in the USA" products. The value of Americans 401K retirement funds has eroded at an astounding pace with no end in sight. The poverty level has reached the highest levels in history. There are more people in the United States on food stamps than ever in the history of America. There are 20,000,000 illegals draining our economy. The national debt has increased to $13.4 trillion. Just how can the mainstream media report that the recession ended in June 2009? We would like to know what they are smoking.

Workers are losing construction jobs in Georgia and manufacturing jobs in Indiana. Some of the layoffs are coming as stimulus money dries up and public works projects come to a halt. Government employees are being let go, too, as states and cities grapple with budget crises.

Without more jobs, consumers will not feel secure enough to spend much money, further slowing the economy. The grim outlook has economists lowering their estimates for growth in the second half of the year.

"Today's news on the economy has been nothing but awful," Paul Ashworth, an economist at Capital Economics, wrote in a note to clients. "The recovery is clearly slowing."

The Labor Department announced Thursday that initial claims for jobless benefits rose by 12,000 last week to 500,000 -- the highest level since November and the third straight increase.

As the economy recovered from the worst downturn since the 1930s, jobless claims declined steadily from a peak of 651,000 in March 2009 to a low of 427,000 in July before rising steadily over the past six weeks. In a healthy economy, jobless claims usually drop below 400,000.

"This is obviously a disappointing number that shows ongoing weakness in the job market," said Robert Dye, senior economist at the PNC Financial Services Group.

Dye said claims showed a similar pattern in the last two recoveries, but eventually began to fall again. The current elevated level of claims is a sign that employers are reluctant to hire until the rebound is well under way. That's what happened after the 1991 and 2001 recessions, which were dubbed "jobless recoveries."

Economists caution that more than 350,000 temporary census jobs ended in recent months, and those workers could be applying for benefits. Congress also recently restored an extended unemployment benefits program, which can sometimes spike claims.

A rush to move money into Treasury's in recent months has sent mortgage rates to the lowest level in decades. They dipped for the eighth time in nine weeks.

Also, the Congressional Budget Office said the deficit is on pace to exceed $1.3 trillion for the budget year that ends in September 2011. That would be the second-largest ever, just below the record of more than $1.4 trillion in the last fiscal year.

Partially fueling the deficit was hundreds of billions of dollars in stimulus spending intended to help lift the country out of recession. But many of the programs are now ending, taking jobs with them.

Ken Simonson, chief economist at the Associated General Contractors of

America, said highway contractors began working on stimulus projects as much as a year ago, "and now that pipeline is empty."

Work on commercial projects such as office buildings, malls and hotels is "dead, dead, dead," he added.

Construction firms are letting go of more workers as the housing sector slumps and federal stimulus spending on public works projects winds down. Construction related layoffs have been particularly heavy in recent weeks in Georgia, Pennsylvania and North Carolina.

In Washington, Republicans have made Democrats' handling of the economy the No. 1 campaign issue heading into the midterm congressional elections. President Barack Obama cited the jump in jobless claims to call attention to Republicans who are opposing his proposal to help small businesses.

That bill would provide up to $30 billion in additional lending to small businesses and about $12 billion in tax breaks to encourage hiring. But Republicans and some Democrats are balking at more government spending because of the effect on the deficit.

The nationwide increase in unemployment claims suggests the economy is creating even fewer jobs than in the first half of this year, when private employers added an average of about 100,000 per month. That's barely enough to keep the unemployment rate from rising. The jobless rate has been stuck at 9.6 percent for two months.

Private employers added only 71,000 jobs in July. But that increase was offset by the loss of 202,000 government jobs, including 143,000 temporary census positions.

July marked the third straight month that the private sector hired cautiously, and economists are concerned that the unemployment rate will start rising again because overall economic growth has weakened significantly since the start of the year.

After expanding at a 3.7 percent annual rate in the first quarter, the economy's growth slowed to 2.4 percent in the April-to-June period. Some economists forecast it will drop as low as 1.5 percent in the third quarter

Does anyone really believe that we are in a recovery? The government keeps revising DOWN the past GDP numbers and jobs reports, sometimes by substantial amounts as well. The April-June quarter is apparently about to get revised down from a GDP of 2.4% to around 1.2% after having taking in to account more recently available data. Similar downward revisions have been on going since the so called recovery began. Now they're revising down future projected growth rates for next year as well.

When you build an economy on a house of cards and provide free benefits to 20%-30% of the populace including illegal migrants what do you really expect. Building on the European model was doomed from the beginning. Like Jack Nicholson said in an old movie, "Keep telling me how good it is...." The 9.6% unemployment figure is a joke. We know the real numbers are more like 20% to 25%. Our future generations are saddled with a debt that can never be paid and now the baby boomers are retiring. Where is the golden goose now? Have you ever heard that the golden goose is cooked?

There was never a recovery, just a delay in the inevitable. The government borrowed money to bail out banks, Wall Street, General Motors, Chrysler, Fannie Mae, Freddie Mac and others, to keep the unemployed eating and with a roof over their head and funding two wars. The United States government has amassed a staggering amount of debt. California, Arizona, Nevada and many, many more are on the verge of default. A nation cannot leverage itself by intentionally moving millions of jobs out of the country

I look at small children and wonder just how difficult life will be for them with all the debt that is being incurred that they will have to someday repay. I know it won't be easy because the current generation has made a mess of what was the greatest nation in the world. We have left the Constitution in ashes as the federal government usurped more and more power from the States in order to be all things to all people. We have created enormous future financial obligations by putting in place entitlement programs which we should have realized were not sustainable.

The government announced more news about their failed economic policies. The private sector is tanking big time. About the only jobs that are created are government funded jobs paid by the taxpayers. Private employers are afraid to hire or expand as they are waiting to see what's in store with the health care and the new financial reform regulation.

While the current administration pretends it has saved millions of jobs that would have been lost if not for the stimulus, there is good reason to believe that in fact millions of people are now unemployed because the stimulus plan has delayed the recovery. The rest of the world is recovering from the global recession far faster than the United States. I suspect this is because their governments eschewed stimulus and many in fact instituted austerity programs - the opposite of stimulus. If we do in fact get the double dip recession that looks increasingly likely, it will be obvious where to lay the blame fro the second dip.

It is funny that the current administration blames Bush, liberals blame Bush, and everyone blames Bush. But it all comes down to the Democrats for blame and failure. They took the congress back in 2004 and got a super majority in 2006. They caused this mess no matter what the administration says and lies about. Mr. Obama was part of the Senate when the Democrats started ruining this country. So if you want blame forget Bush. This is all a Democrat mess we are in. Only if you believe their lies will you see otherwise.

The majority of the economist predicted this back in February 2009, when the President and the Democrats rammed their stimulus package down America's throat. If they were going to spend 787 billion dollars that we did not have they should have given it directly to small business owners in the form of very low interest loans so those businesses could keep and hire more employees. Instead they threw it all at wasteful government spending while they were passing new laws (Healthcare) that did nothing but add to costs for many businesses.

Our economy is in the quick sand and the President and Chairman of the Board of General Motors are going to be spending $500 million to expand a General Motors plant in Mexico. This is a company that we bailed out to the tune of $50 Billion and that the government owns 61% of the company. How does this administration explain a company it owns taking taxpayer money to expand its foreign operations. Why isn't General Motors going to expand in Detroit? Jobs are leaving the United States because of moves like this and the governments anti-business mentality. General Motors should have their payroll in Mexico taxed a rate of 75% of the gross wages paid.

It should be noted that when the democrats took over congress in January 2006, gas was $1.89 a gallon, unemployment was 4.8%, the national debt was $9 Trillion and the largest deficit in history at that time was $400 Billion.

Yes, I'll take a 3/5 majority in Congress to raise the National Debt any day over this disgusting, wasteful and intolerable spending that is an insult to the American Taxpayer, the American people, the American economy and all free people of the world.

My Fellow Americans, the challenges that our nation faces are not rocket science, we just need leadership that can explain those challenges in a little more detail, with a little more explanation about the struggle that we will endure and the ultimate outcome that will make our nation strong and prosperous.....simply, logically and with a little Common Sense.

Once the Balanced Budget Amendment is enacted, I guarantee you that everyone's attention will be focused on finding solutions, and quickly, because Congress, in its infinite wisdom, will no longer be able to borrow money without a 3/5 majority in both houses of Congress to raise the National Debt.

Maybe if our government would stop giving away money we don't have to foreign countries whenever they fail to handle their own crisis situations. We have our own crisis here at home. Our Citizens and States need that aid money that the government is sending abroad. Why should America borrow money from China just to give it away overseas? Let someone else be the world's deep pockets for a change. You don't see China giving much money to the United Nations, Pakistan, etc even though they could afford it.

The Democrats are also not off the hook. Bill Clinton signed into law the Gramm-Leach-Bliley act in 1999 and the vast majority of Democrats voted for it. Barney Frank and friends pushed so hard for more bad loans to be written to the indigent and minorities who did not have a prayers chance of making payments full term. This created more bad derivative products and more leverage and more trouble placing positions well over the edge.

Believe it or not President Bush tried to warn and stop this but was beaten down as being against the under privileged. The immigration problem is largely to be blamed on Democrats who pander to ethnic lobbyists against the needs of the United States.

The current administration has been working very hard for the last twenty four months. They have blamed the prior administrations for all the current problems. It is time that the present administration steps up to the plate and admits that they have a majority in both houses and are just trying to cram programs down the American citizens throat that the majority do not want. The current administration has increased our federal deficit by approximately $4 trillion all while going on extended vacations and sending their family to foreign countries. Their plan to pass job destroying plans is working very successfully since we have a real unemployment figure in the range of 20% to 25% when we count everyone whose unemployment benefits have expired, those that do not qualify for unemployment benefits, and those Americans that have just given up.

The current elevated level of claims is a sign employers are reluctant to hire until the rebound is well under way. When companies need people they will only hire if they are able to show investors a profit for several consecutive quarters. Earnings have been spotty for many companies and reductions in employees are one way they can reduce their expenses. If you have a bad quarter and it looks like the same for the next quarter then you have layoffs. Companies need to show a profit for investors to invest and to get bank loans. Companies do not wait for a rebound. They respond to their needs and the needs of their customers when they hire. Right now the demand of products and services is low. Until the public and companies start spending again, we are in for a long haul.

The current administrations policies will never work. The government has spent $787 billion of the taxpayer's money on a stimulus program that has been a total disaster. Wake up and admit that the government can not spend us out of this current recession. I think it is really a depression.

The administration has to develop legislation that does not punish business expecting to achieve favorable results. We need to extent the Bush tax cuts for at least 5 years until this current financial mess is resolved.

CHAPTER FIFTEEN

The Budget and Deficit

The government must be required to balance the budget and eliminate the deficit spending policies that have created approximately $13.4 trillion in federal deficit.

The following is printed from the Constitution of the United States of America.

The Constitution of the United States

Section 7 - Revenue Bills, Legislative Process, Presidential Veto

All bills for raising Revenue shall originate in the House of Representatives; but the Senate may propose or concur with Amendments as on other Bills.

Every Bill which shall have passed the House of Representatives and the Senate, shall, before it become a Law, be presented to the President of the United States; If he approve he shall sign it, but if not he shall return it, with his Objections to that House in which it shall have originated, who shall enter the Objections at large on their Journal, and proceed to reconsider it. If after such Reconsideration two thirds of that House shall agree to pass the Bill, it shall be sent, together with the Objections, to the other House, by which it shall likewise be reconsidered, and if approved by two thirds of that House, it shall become a Law. But in all such Cases the Votes of both Houses shall be determined by Yeas and Nays, and the Names of the Persons voting for and against the Bill shall be entered on the Journal of each House respectively. If any Bill shall not be returned by the President within ten Days (Sundays excepted) after it shall have been presented to him, the Same shall be a Law, in like Manner as if he had signed it, unless the Congress by their Adjournment prevent its Return, in which Case it shall not be a Law.

Every Order, Resolution, or Vote to which the Concurrence of the Senate and House of Representatives may be necessary (except on a question of Adjournment) shall be presented to the President of the United States; and before the Same shall take Effect, shall be approved by him, or being disapproved by him, shall be re-passed by two thirds of the Senate and House of Representatives, according to the Rules and Limitations prescribed in the Case of a Bill.

When is the federal government going to realize that they have to prepare an annual budget? On October 1, 2010 the government will be operating without an annual budget that has been approved by Congress.

PAYING OFF THE NATIONAL DEBT WILL NOT HAPPEN WITH THE SPENDING POLICIES OF THIS PRESIDENT

In 2010 (latest data available, source: Wikipedia),

Revenues of the Federal Government are budgeted at $2.381 Trillion:

45% - Personal Income Taxes --- $1,061B

40% - Social Security and Medicare --- $940B

9% - Corporate Taxes --- $222B

6% - Other --- $158B

Expenditures of the Federal Government are budgeted at $3.6 Trillion:

28.9% --- Entitlement Programs --- $1,040.4B

19.6% --- Social Security --- $705.6B

16.1% --- Unemployment/Welfare/Other --- $579.6B

12.8% --- Medicare --- $460.8B

8.2% --- Medicaid & SCHIP --- $295.2B

9.0% --- National Defense --- $324.0B

3.5% --- Interest on the National Debt --- $126.0B

1.9% --- Discretionary Spending --- $69.3B

A deficit (shortage) of $1.219 Trillion dollars to be added to the $13.4 Trillion National Debt we already have now!

In a June 9, 2009 New York Times article David Leonhardt wrote "Mr. Obama does not have a realistic plan for eliminating the deficit." And this is from the New York Times! If the New York Times is reporting that the president is clueless we must really be in trouble.

The current administration, led by President Obama tries to sell the United States on the theory that deficit spending will cure the economic problems. Just how does he ever plan on paying this deficit off? Look out America, this President thinks raising taxes in going to be the answer.

Obama lacerates over exploding deficits? Since the Democrats have controlled both houses (including the last two years of Bush term) the deficit has totally exploded - Don't blame the people who were not in power. If Congress did not want deficits - then it would have done something with their spending habits.

The Economy

The economy of the United States has reached unbearable levels and needs to have the politicians take drastic measures and get it back on the right track. The Democrats are of the belief that the Bush tax cuts need to be extended only for the middle class taxpayers. They do not understand that the rates should be renewed for every American. There should not be any program that institutes a class structure in the United States of America. The Republicans realize that higher tax rates would hurt small businesses and the job creation that the economy is badly in need of is stymied. Job creation is desperately needed as the economy is suffering from its worst recession since the 1930's.

The House Speaker Nancy Pelosi was under extreme pressure to send the Democrats home to campaign with the strongest possible closing argument. Pelosi is considering calling a vote on extending middle-class tax cuts. This is a blatant attempt to sway voters by portraying the Republican Party as trying to protect the richer taxpayers. What the Democrats do not understand is that there should not be any class structure in the United States. House Democrats were trying desperately to maintain control of the House of Representatives and are looking at any means to accomplish that mission. Thank the American voters for making sure that the Republicans gained control of the House of Representatives and made major inroads into the Senate. Pelosi attempts to bully the members to have a vote before the elections due to the fact that their chances of success will be eroding after the upcoming elections. There are already 30 Democrats that do not believe it advantageous to hold the vote on the Bush tax cuts prior to the election. The sheep are leaving the flock to try to save their own jobs. If Congress does not act before December 31, 2010 the Bush tax cuts will expire and every American will have a tax increase of some sort.

For those of you who think that the rich don't pay any taxes at all.

Here are some facts for you: The top 1% paid 40% of all taxes. The top 5% paid 60% of all taxes. The top 10% paid 71% of all taxes. The top 25% paid 86% of all taxes. The top 50% paid 97% of all taxes. The sad truth is that 50% of all taxpayers did not pay any income taxes. This information comes from Internal Revenue Service data. With the top 1% paying about 40% of all income taxes paid to the Internal Revenue Service they should also get a break with the extension of the Bush tax cuts.

The Congress went home without stopping the tax hike on American families and small businesses. By doing that would wallop every taxpayer with a tax hike in a struggling economy — and that's simply irresponsible.

Of course Obama was lying about taxes. How is he suppose to pay for all that amazing health care reform, borrowing, spending, bailouts and printing money that he has been doing since day one? The problem is that people are not taking this seriously. Increase taxes and good luck finding a job. Already businesses are wondering what is coming with all the new laws and regulations from the healthcare reform and financial regulations. They are stocking away money, not hiring. If you are going to be looking for a new job over the next few years you will need good luck. And if the government ends the tax cuts, cuts back on itemized deductions, etc., you will see many more people cutting their costs. And even more hardship on folks that depend on donations from these people. Things are going to get much worse before they get better we will have to hit the bottom first. Oust the idiots in Washington and take our government back.

Anyone that thinks increasing those taxes on businesses will produce jobs has absolutely no clue about running a business. The facts are that businesses already pay a 35% corporate tax rate. Businesses already pay from 2 to 10 times as much for the same property in property taxes. Businesses pay all your unemployment insurance premiums. Businesses pay all your workmen's compensation insurance. Businesses pay from 75% to 100% of health care insurance. Businesses pay 11% of your wages in social security taxes. Businesses pay a lot and you want them to pay more and you expect job growth ... you have absolutely no clue about running a business. That is where Obama is coming from. We need to elect the next president and members of Congress that have some idea about building and running a business. Possibly then we will see the unemployment rates go back down where they need to be for our economy to recover.

When we cut the government spending and reduce earmark spending we will see the economy improve. We can not continue to spend what we do not have and expect the taxpayers to ante up more taxes to cover the recklessness of the politicians in Washington. An example of the duplicate spending and waste would be the National Public Radio. It was created in case of a national emergency. We do not need it any more since we have the Emergency Broadcast System in which every radio and television station is required to participate in. Cut the funding for the National Public Radio it is nothing but total waste.

There is no need for the taxpayers to fund the National Education Association. There are state associations, local associations, school boards, parent teacher associations that can perform the same functions. What do they do, fund the free lunch program? Can't those duties be passed to the state level causing there to be no need for $200 thousand per year administrators at the federal level who do nothing then bust the balls of the state administrators in the first place. Cut all funding to the National Education Association. The duplication is nothing but total waste.

I guess the moral of the story is that if buggy whips were funded by the federal government, we'd all still be driving horse drawn buggies and we would need a buggy whip. It's time to move into the information age and cut the waste from government.

The tax cuts were enacted in 2001 and 2003 after Bush made them the centerpiece of his election campaign. They provided help for rich and poor alike. The Democrats are always crying the tax cuts were only for the rich. By the way, one of the tax cuts of the Bush plan was to have a reduction in the "Marriage Penalty". If this is repealed, a married couple, each with an income of $30,000 a year will pay $5,000 more in income taxes. Is that what the taxpayer really wants? I do not know if it applies to same-sex marriages.

So, Obama campaigned on how the Bush tax cuts ruined this economy and how he would get rid of them as they only take care of the rich and people bought into it. Now, the Democrats are considering extending the Bush tax cuts only for the people earning under $200 thousand per year during a time when the economy is so fragile. The Bush tax cuts affect us all and the middle class will feel it if they are left to expire. There will be higher income taxes and no deductions which will mean less money in your pocket. Thank Bush for those cuts you all enjoyed. It is sad that some thought the rich are the only ones benefiting.

The United States of America is struggling with the economy and some of the things that could help fix the problem are:

I would recommend legislation that would impose a tariff on all goods that are imported from Mexico, Canada, China, Japan and any other country that is importing more goods into the United States than we are exporting goods to their country.

We need to establish an American policy that we will not have any more deficits of foreign trade. We need to operate within a balance budget.

The government needs to start taxing all corporate profits no matter where the income is earned for the corporation. This will eliminate any accounting practices that are designed to move income from one country to another to evade income taxes.

It would be nice to see legislation that puts an immediate pay reduction to every government employee in the amount of 25% of their gross earning. It seems like the government employees have been given raises while the Senior Citizens and other recipients of Social Security have been placed on a freeze of benefits. The average wage of the government employee is about 65% higher than an employee doing the same type job in the private sector. This will reduce the budget deficit immediately.

The United States needs to rescind the NAFTA. The United States will not stop hemorrhaging jobs until we make it economical to build factories here again. We need to tax imports at the same rate that United States products are taxed in their country. The United States needs to mandate that all government and military contracts are awarded to United States companies and the work be completed in the United States.

The United States needs to pass legislation reestablishing the Investment Tax Credit. This will give employers an immediate income tax credit equal to 15% on all depreciable assets with a useful life of 10 years or longer. This will encourage employers to build facilities in the United States.

Well, the mainstream is pulling out all stops to paint the Democrats as the savior to the world. When will they wake up? This article was posted on Yahoo and was written by the Associated Press on September 18, 2010.

A Democratic pollster said, "People are trying to figure out what happened to our economy and how do we improve our economy," adding that in their view "you have to get back to policies that really encourage manufacturing in America and making things in America." Now that is something that the Democrats should have tried to understand when the NAFTA was passed? The NAFTA was a big giant mess that did not help the American businesses in any way. Now the American public can see what a disgrace it has been. We can thank President Clinton for that. It is amazing just how short the Democrats memory really is.

In California, where unemployment stood at 12.3 percent in July, Senator Barbara Boxer recently began running a commercial that says Republican candidate Carly Fiorina laid off 30,000 workers while she was CEO of computer giant Hewlett-Packard. We wonder just how many of those jobs were for union employees. Could it be that if all the unions were done away with how many more jobs would be created and just how many jobs would not have to be outsourced to another country when our labor costs would become competitive?

What the Democrats are failing to disclose is that during Barbara Boxer's time in Congress that she has voted for more than $1 trillion in higher taxes on the hard working Americans. Boxer has been a major supporter of job killing legislation that has crippled small businesses. In addition, Boxer has voted many times on legislation that increased our national debt to historic levels.

The Democrats need to stop bashing the Republican opponents if they have any intention of retaining control of the House of Representatives or Congress. The American voters are very tired of the rhetoric pointing the blame for everything on every one else except themselves. The voting public is not going to believe any of the garbage that is spewing out of the Democrats mouths. Get a platform about what you are going to do for America. Remember, ask not what your country can do for you. Ask what you can do for your country. It is past time for all of the politicians to stop thinking about keeping their jobs.

Democratic campaign committees commissioned surveys to measure the impact of the issue nationally, and have urged individual candidates to incorporate it into their campaigns. They said the surveys found that an allegation of outsourcing was most effective when leveled against a candidate who had a personal connection to the migration of jobs overseas, as a businessman, for example. In other cases, including races in Wisconsin, Illinois, Nevada, Virginia and elsewhere, Democrats have seized on a no-tax-increase pledge signed by Republican incumbents or candidates as evidence they want to protect breaks for companies that export jobs. Then there are the allegations that a Republican will support a new trade deal sending jobs overseas. What happened to the Democrats memories? It was the Clinton administration that created the NAFTA which is responsible for sending jobs to other countries. Just once it would be so refreshing to hear a Democrat make an election speech where they would present a program that will bring the unemployment down and improve the economy. All they can preach is who caused the past.

Give the American taxpayer something to believe in like more job opportunities and lower taxes. Stimulate the economy instead of creating more benefits for the unions.

Stop blocking legislation to limit the amount of money corporations and unions can spend on campaign advertising, President Barack Obama is telling Republicans, saying their strategy is "politics at its worst." That is a quote from the Associated Press. Now that is pathetic since it was reported that the unions had committed to spend $50 million to support the Democrats that were having trouble during the mid-term elections in November. Obama needs to spend more time learning about government for the people instead of playing basketball. Obama stated "this is common sense". You have to be kidding.

After you have the money it is time to restrict how much money the others can have. This is real class? When this economy is in that tank like it is Obama wants to take the time to discuss and argue about raising money for the elections.

Would it be better to spend this time presenting proposals that will help solve the problems we have with the economy, taxes, unemployment and the deficit. Not to mention that the poverty rate in the United States has increased to 14.3% which is the highest level since 1965?

The Democrats are once again spending their time focusing on the partisan effort to rig the fall elections rather than the stagnant economy. The Democrats are proving once again that the jobs they care about most are their own. This is just another transparent effort to try and help themselves ahead of an election in which they clearly can't run on their record. The Obama administration needs to understand that they need to freeze government spending and stop any tax hikes scheduled to take effect on January 1, 2011. Congress needs to intervene to make sure that all Americans enjoy the current tax structure. How can the Democrats even think about raising taxes with the economy in the state that it is?

That is where the problem lies. This administration does not have any proposals that will change the unemployment problem or fix the economy. As for the deficit the only proposals that are presented are to increase spending without showing any possible way to pay for it except increase the deficit. The idea to change the way the contribution system works at this point in time is nothing more than trying to portray the Republicans as not wanting to vote on the Democratic bills. It should be pointed out that the Democrats have 59 seats in the Congress and the Republicans only have 39. There are 2 Independents. The Democrats have 255 representatives in the House of Representatives and the Republicans have 178. There should not be any reason that the Obama administration couldn't pass the legislation that they were proposing. All the Obama administration needs to do is present legislation that is for the best of all Americans. When that happens there will be bipartisanship in both houses. The majority of the programs that have finally been passed were basically crammed down the throats of the voting public. The majority of the voters have been against all the major legislation that has been enacted. The Obama and crew have increased the deficit more in 25 months than any president in the history of the United States.

Reports have been published that the $787 billion stimulus funds used $70 million in Los Angeles, California to create 7 new jobs. We are wondering just how that was a positive program to eliminate unemployment and stimulate the economy? The Department of Transportation created or retained 9 jobs with their $40 million in stimulus money.

The same audit reported the waste that was involved in these stimulus funds. The Department of Transportation, for instance, spent $9 million to install new LED light bulbs in traffic lights at 1,800 intersections. Less the $228,000 in labor costs associated with the project, that's nearly $5,000 per location to change light bulbs. Another project spent $4 million to install 65 new left-turn arrows, averaging more than $61,500 per arrow. How can Obama consider such wasteful spending to be good for the economy and prudent? This is just another example showing that Obama does not have a clue about running a business let alone America.

CHAPTER SIXTEEN

Plum Island

Plum Island has been a research center since the 1950s. Scientists have studied dangerous animal diseases on the island that if unleashed could imperil the nation's livestock. Cold War germ warfare testing also occurred on Plum Island, and for decades the United States Army used it as a coastal defense post.

Reports are that Plum Island is going to be put up for sale. How can the government even think about turning this contaminated island in the hands of private citizens? The island is a remarkable location for fish and wildlife. Let them have it.

If the government really would like to do something worthwhile with the island they should make it into a federal prison that could be used to house all the prisoners that have been given a life sentence.

What is really shocking is that the federal government would like to relocate the animal disease lab to the center of Kansas and they are proceeding with their plan to sell the island. The island contains 840 acres and is located off the eastern tip of Long Island. What on earth are they thinking about? It is absolutely insane to even think about putting a hazardous animal disease facility in the heart of cattle country. There could be a potential disaster greater than the Gulf oil spill or hurricane Katrina. Not to mention that Kansas is also in one of the country's tornado belts. This is a disaster waiting to happen.

Also under way is a congressional risk assessment of Homeland Security's decision to move the animal disease lab to Manhattan, Kansas. Some lawmakers question the wisdom of studying dangerous pathogens in the so-called Beef Belt. The Department of Homeland Security has determined that an accidental release of foot-and-mouth disease would have a $4.2 billion impact on the economy, regardless of the lab's location.

Reports are that Plum Island could fetch a price as high as $50 million. That would not even cover the cost of the government getting the island into marketable condition. The remaining cleanup cost for the island would exceed the sale price. In addition to the laboratory the island features a water filtration plant, sewage treatment facilities and other amenities that would make it an ideal site for a federal prison. Security would be easy to establish and the facilities could be used for administration of the prison.

The Government Accounting Office stated that Plum Island scientists did research on such pathogens as foot and mouth disease, which is highly contagious to livestock and could cause catastrophic economic losses and imperil the nation's food supply. Now the government wants to move the research center of an island where a contamination can be controlled and place it in Kansas. Don't the government know about Kansas livestock? It is quite apparent that our government is still full of people that do not have an ounce of common sense. Not to mention the staggering costs to move the facility. Projections are $600 million to build the facility. The plan for a bio building only costs $32 million and how much is it gong to cost to move all those scientists to Kansas? That is if they will even move there. For once will the government at least try to make it look like they are being frugal with the taxpayer's money? Was this a pork project for the Senators from Kansas? Did the entire Senate actually vote on this proposal?

It doesn't matter how many times I try to understand this move it just doesn't make any sense. The Plum Island facility was a secluded area that was surrounded by water that has a facility that can provide everything required for the research and they want to move into the heart of our country. They have been studying some of the most dangerous diseases in the world at the facility and now they want to move to the center of the country with no barriers.

Wow, this part of Kansas is full of feedlots and meatpacking plants. It smells so disgusting and is such big business, it seems like the meat industry owns most of this area. It is so abusive to the land, air, and people...oh yeah, and the cows too.

Sure looks like an area where want dangerous diseases tested.

CHAPTER SEVENTEEN

The Too Big to Fail Policy

Where did the federal government come up with the idea that businesses were to large to fail? The size of the business should not have any bearing on whether if succeeds or fails. If they run their business properly it will be a success. If they fail to run the business it should be allowed to fail. There should not be any exceptions.

The Obama administration was promoting this idea to the American public so that he could press for the immediate consolidation of some of the major companies in the United States. The reason that Bank of America was forced into acquiring Merrill Lynch and Countrywide Home Loans was to show the world that Obama could dictate to business what it has to do. These companies will stand up and deny that they were basically told to do the mergers or else. This was just another example of the Chicago style back room politics.

Merrill Lynch should have filed for reorganization under the current bankruptcy laws of the United States. Instead they were acquired by Bank of America in what turned out to be a very suspect transaction. Where was the proxy statement from Merrill Lynch to its shareholders that would have required a vote to pass the merger? Where was the proxy statement of the Bank of America that would have received the shareholder approval for the merger? Due to the time frame of this acquisition there could not have been any input from the shareholders with regard to the merger. The same thing should have been done in the Countrywide Home Loans acquisition.

The federal government needs to stop meddling in the business affairs of corporate America or any business for that matter.

Now we need to examine the General Motors Corp. and the Chrysler Corp. bailouts by the United States government and foreign countries. This was an absolute disgrace to the shareholders of both companies. The government forced these companies into structured bankruptcies without any input from the shareholders of either company. There are certain policies and procedures that must be followed in the corporate world. Notifying the shareholders of impending problems is one of them. The shareholders were not given proper notification that these companies were on the verge of cutting their throats. Had the required filings been made the shareholders would have had a chance to liquidate their shares instead of ending up with a worthless piece of paper.

The shareholders of General Motors and Chrysler deserved better treatment from the government pressure that was placed upon the companies.

Had the government allowed the businesses to take the normal course of action they would have filed for reorganization under the bankruptcy codes and then the government could have provided them with some debtor financing until the reorganization process was completed. What more than likely would have happened is that the bankruptcy courts would have required the abandonment of the unions as part of the reorganization plans? Contrary to what the government was stating that it would put many companies out of business that was to help promote the fact that Obama wanted to save the unions. Without the unions both of these companies could have restructured into companies that could compete with wages that provided a good living for the employees. The trickle down effect would have been that all the parts manufacturers and suppliers would have also had to dissolve the unions. The only ones that this would irritate would be the union employees but they could have been given the rights to be considered for hire before anyone else. The problem that the unions would have with this is that their employees are not always the highest qualified or most dependable.

The bankruptcy courts could have demanded that the pension fund financing be reworked along with all the other debts of the companies. There has never been a government program in the history of America that has ruined the lives of so many Americans and then had the audacity to try and sell the people that it was best for them.

The government made sure that the unions were going to be voting for him and the Democrats in the future. I agree that the unions had a great place in American history and were good for the country. Unfortunately, the time has passed for the country to need them and they have played a major part in ruining America during the past two decades. They are like dinosaurs and should be made extinct. That goes for all the unions. Every employee should be paid on the merits of the work that they provide their employer. When they are exceptional they deserve a bonus. When they are inferior they deserve to be fired. Unfortunately, it is going to be a very hard sell to abolish the unions. When it happens there will be more employment because the overpayment of the union employees will stop and the companies can pay the wages that are realistic to more people. There will be a lot more workers and fewer supervisors.

The American people are hurting. As a result of the greed, recklessness and illegal behavior on Wall Street, millions of Americans have lost their jobs, homes, life savings and their ability to get a higher education. Today, some 22 percent of our children live in poverty, and 48.1 million have become dependent on food stamps for their food.

Today, because of stagnating wages and higher costs for basic necessities, the average two-wage-earner family has less disposable income than a one-wage-earner family did a generation ago. The average American today is underpaid, overworked and stressed out as to what the future will bring for his or her children. For many, the American dream has become a nightmare. The government is trying to destroy a strong middle class which is what made the United States the envy of the world. In its place they are determined to create an oligarchy in which a small number of families control the economic and political life of our country.

Last year, the top twenty-five hedge fund managers made a combined $25 billion but because of tax policy their lobbyists helped write, they pay a lower effective tax rate than many teachers, nurses and police officers. As a result of tax havens in the Cayman Islands, Bermuda and elsewhere, the wealthy and large corporations are evading some $100 billion a year in United States income taxes. Warren Buffet, one of the richest people on earth, has often bragged that he pays a lower effective tax rate than his secretary.

But it's not just wealthy individuals who grotesquely manipulate the system for their benefit. It's the multinational corporations they own and control. In 2009, Exxon Mobil, the most profitable corporation in history made $19 billion in profits and not only paid no federal income tax—they actually received a $156 million refund from the government. In 2005, one out of every four large corporations in the United States paid no federal income taxes while earning $1.1 trillion in revenue.

This is an example of failing no matter what the size.

CHAPTER EIGHTEEN

The Effect of Illegals in America

The major affect that the illegals have in America is to try and destroy our standard of living and turn our beautiful country into another third world country that does not seem to care whether it is kept clean and respectful. How dare they come into our country and demand the same rights as the American citizens and the legal immigrants. Americans work very hard to preserve our freedoms and protect our rights. We do not appreciate the fact that the illegals grab the Mexican flag and do protest marches against our country because we do not want to make them citizens.

There are thousands of illegals marching through out southern border every week. They do not have any fear of the border patrol and leave miles of garbage strewn all over the Arizona Desert. It is outrageous that our federal government does not enforce the laws of our country. We need to contact every representative and make sure that they vote to stop amnesty and finish the construction of the border fence. There can not be any amnesty if we want America to return to "America the Beautiful"

The following statistics have been presented by the local ranchers who observed the situation first hand. They did not use the government statistics but kept track of the local incidents. What the residents found was that they were involved in the capture on one bunch of illegals at one time. They did not bother with the countless small groups. They found loads of drugs and captured 213 illegals. They had dangerous encounters with illegals on 132 separate occasions. There were 16 dead illegals that were found by civilians in the area. In the last year there were 14 high speed chases between dope haulers and law enforcement. Fires that were started by these illegals happened 9 times and over 100,000 acres were burned costing the taxpayers $40 million dollars. One fire in Portal, Arizona in June 2010 cost the taxpayers $10 million to fight according to estimates of the forest service.

There also have been some outlandish incidents one of which was a bachelor in the Portal area was burglarized around 100 times. He finally took all his valuables and put them in a steel vault and welded the door shut. He then moved out of his house into a shed hoping the illegal aliens would leave him alone. They did not and he finally had to abandon his property. Another outlandish event was when outlaws stole a brand new Caterpillar motor grader on the Geronimo Trail east of Douglas, Arizona and drove south through the border fence never to be seen again. The grader belonged to Cochise County Hwy Dept.

It is estimated that the financial losses to private sector – exceed $100,000,000 in the value of real estate, personal property, loss of wildlife habitat among a few. We need to secure our border and deport all the illegals. We do not want to become a third world country.

The area we are reviewing is an area that covers approximately 17 or 18 townships with only 20 miles being adjacent to the US - Mexico Boundary. Within this area, there is a population of perhaps 600 people, 90% of which reside in Rodeo, New Mexico or Portal, Arizona 30 miles or so north of Mexico. No less than 80% of the people in this area have been burglarized or otherwise molested by illegal aliens.

Unless you have witnessed first hand what is going on at the borders of the Unites States you don't understand just how serious the problems of these illegals are. The photo below could help you understand who might be your new neighbor in a couple of days.

There is a billboard close to the Arizona border that says it all about the feelings of the Arizona citizens.

"Attention Illegal Immigrants"

Arizona does not welcome you, but Los Angeles loves you.

Free Housing, Free School, Free Food, Free Medical, and

Free Hospital.

No Insurance Costs, no taxes, and plenty of jobs.

TURN LEFT ON I-8 AND FOLLOW YOUR ROAD TO PARADISE!

The illegal immigrant problem is not limited to the federal government. The state of California is facing a $19 billion deficit for the current fiscal year. If California was not supporting 10.8 million illegals they would have a balanced budget. There would not be rampant unemployment and the social services departments would not be overloaded with payments to these illegals. The amount that California is spending to support these illegals is much higher that the $1,759.30 that each of them would save the state of California. We all know that it is costing the state many times that amount to support each of these illegals. Anything over the $1,759.30 per individual that the state of California would save would contribute to a surplus. Why is it that the Governor of California is against deporting the illegals? Sure would make the state of California much better off financially. After all we can't offend the poor Mexicans that are destroying our way of life. It might also offend the ACLU and the other special interest groups. Who would the Democratic Party have left to vote for them?

For centuries the American people have welcomed individuals from all over the world. The difference is that these immigrants did it legally. Does any understand the difference? The legal immigrants tent to respect the laws of our great country while the illegals are criminals that have started their lives in America by breaking the law. For generations people have wanted to come to America and wanted to end up being citizens of the great country. They have waited the five year waiting period and taken the tests required to become citizens. These immigrants have been sworn in as citizens in front of the flag of the United States and appreciate with all their heart that America has let them become citizens.

On the other hand we have the illegals that cross over the border under the cover of darkness and in many cases carrying a backpack full of illegal drugs. The fact that our government has not enforced the laws of our country is an absolute disgrace to the citizens of the United States.

It is hard to understand why the federal government does not want to accept the fact that the Mexican's are actually in a war with the United States. They have invaded our country with 20 million people, many of whom carry weapons. We need to wake up America and start standing up for our rights. Does anyone really think that there is another country in the world that would let 20 million people invade their nations?

Then we see on the news that the United Nations is looking into the actions of our individual states. The report from a representative of the United Nations said "Arizona's new immigration law, passed to expel nearly half a million illegal immigrants from the state and stem the flow of human drug smugglers over the border from Mexico was certain to be raised at an international conference on migration in Mexico in November."

The South African jurist said the Global Forum on Migration and Development, an annual United Nations initiative, would discuss the measure, which United Nation officials have already denounced as discriminatory because it allows police to stop and search individuals on the suspicion they are illegal immigrants.

The people of the United States need to declare the war and let the United Nations know that when they show that one of their countries will allow 20 million illegal immigrants to enter without papers we will too. You can bet anything you own that there will be a different attitude when it comes to their countries.

On October 3, 2010 the Denver Post reported that a couple enjoying a lake on the Texas Mexico border had to dodge gunfire from pirates on the lake.

The wife was forced to make an impossible choice: risk her life by staying with her husband or return to land and seek help.

The couple was sightseeing on Jet Skis on the Mexican side of Falcon Lake when several boats of gunmen opened fire, striking her husband in the back of his head. According to the 911 call released reports from law enforcement officials detail the tragic incident.

The woman was seeing bullets hitting close to her in the water and realized that her husband had been hit behind the head. She went back trying to find, trying to help him. She went in the water trying to load up her husband to her Jet Ski trying to get his body and Jet Ski back to the United States side. She was being shot at so she finally had to let go of the body, climb back in her Jet Ski and head back over here to the United States. The woman said that the armed men believed to be pirates associated with a Mexican drug cartel, chased her into United States waters as she fled.

The lake is not secure, the border is not secure because the incident we were dreading the most has in fact happened. We cannot go to Mexico, we cannot recover that body, we cannot conduct an investigation and we have to tell the family we can't do anything about it.

Although it was only one couple of Americans it is still an act of war against the citizens of the United States and should be treated as such. We will have to wait and see what our President is going to do about this incident. More than likely he will scold the woman for enjoying the lake.

Why the members of Congress are not proposing legislation to stop this insane policy of allowing the illegals to remain in our country is nothing more that lack of respect for the country that they represent. I published a list of the Congressional members that voted to allow the illegals to receive social security benefits and the members that voted against making English the official language of the United States. It seems to me that that was what the founders of America wanted and that the requirement is in the Constitution.

These illegals sneak into the United States under the cover of darkness and then feel that they have more rights and considerations than an American citizen. That is what the liberals of our once proud country have done to the good citizens. The politicians want to make these people legal instead of deporting them solely for the purpose of obtaining their votes. Why then are some of the Republicans looking out for the illegals? They should realize that the vast majority of the illegals will be voting Democratic.

The effect of the illegals in the United State can be measured in many ways. We are going to look at some of the problems that are caused by the 20 million illegals that are living in the United States of America.

The American people need to realize just how much the illegal population in the United States is costing us in terms of real dollars and supporting costs caused by the entitlement programs that have been provided by the government.

How about computing some real costs for the 20 million illegals in the country? First, if these illegals are working they will probably be earning in the $6 to $10 thousand range per year. Most of them will be supporting their families and have on average two children. OK?

We will use the $10 thousand per year income to make the numbers easier to work with. Let's assume that there are 3,000,000 families that would fall into this category. The fact that most of these are working illegally they will not be paying anything into the government such as social security and Medicare deductions from their wages. Then these 3 million families file a tax return because they know from all of their other illegals that the government will give them an earned income credit that will provide them with a refund of about $3,200 per family. That does not sound like a huge amount of money but how about multiplying it over the 3 million people. It is a cash outlay to the federal government of $9,600,000,000. That is right, $9.6 billion.

When we compute the average of the entitlement programs that these illegals are receiving the cost is going to go up by an astounding amount. These entitlements will cost the tax-payers on average $22 per illegal that is in the United States. That figure is for every one of the 20 million illegals and would cost the government $4,400,000,000. With just these two items we could cut our budget deficit by $14 billion dollars per year.

I recommend that the federal government pass legislation that would set up a super fund for deportation and construction of the fence to secure the borders in the amount of $25 billion. In the proposed federal budget for the year there is a provision for 20,000 troops. How many are we really expecting to see on the border? This fund would be used to hire as many employees as it needs to deport the 20 million illegals that are draining our resources. The government would save many times that amount during the first two years and we would have the problem solved. This fund would also be used to complete our border security so that we do not have the problem again. The government does not want the border secured is where the problem comes from. Going back to the 2011 proposed budget there are already funds allocated to hire an additional 20,000 border support personnel. Somewhere along the way these troops have been only a figment of Obama's imagination. They are no where to be seen on the border between Arizona and Mexico. These funds would be returned to the United States economy due to the fact that the 20 million illegals would not be able to send $35 to $50 billion in American money back to Mexico.

I know that this would create some government spending but it would also pave the way for balancing the budget in the next and future years. I am only for spending that can be recovered by the savings that will be generated by the legislation. This proposal is a situation where every American will benefit and the government will be saving money and resources for years to come. We will be balancing the annual budget and creating millions of jobs with the same legislation. A balanced budget and creation of jobs is what the American people want, isn't it?

You can already hear the ACLU and other organizations that always screaming about these illegals civil rights. Of course that is the only thing they care about and not the recovery of the United States. Why do they want to turn our beautiful country into a third world mess such as Mexico?

Now we will try to compute some of the resources that the government is spending because of these 20 million illegals. The cost of incarceration alone cost the government $1.095 trillion per year. Welfare and social services for these illegals is costing the government $90 billion per year. The American workers are being denied access to $200 billion per year in wages that are taken by these illegals. Trying to be conservative these expenditures are causing an increase in the federal deficit every year in the amount of $1.385 trillion. Not even taking into consideration the lost wages for the American people.

The following steps were recommended by others but they reflect my feelings accurately and should be those of the entire United States. We need to close the border with Mexico. The President's proposed budget has included 20,000 troops that could be utilized for that purpose. This will provide instant relief to our local communities, state social services, federal social services, hospitals, schools, jails and federal prisons. We need to make E-verify a universal law and the employers that do not verify must be held accountable and fined $50,000 per infraction.

Every illegal that is living in the United States should be given a 30 day grace period to get their possessions in order and go back over the border. Those that do not choose to leave will be arrested and prosecuted for violating the law of the United States by entering our country illegally. If they are arrested the government will be authorized to seize all of their property.

Any illegal that is receiving public money or any other kind of support from the federal, state, or local authorities will cease to receive any funds immediately. There are over 20 million illegals in the United States and we need to stop providing shelter, jobs and any other support. These illegals are taking over 10 million jobs from the American people.

Every legal citizen needs to prepare for the next new neighbor that comes parading across the southern border. They just might move in next door.

CHAPTER NINETEEN

The Foreign Labor Costs

How do the manufacturers in the United States justify having their production plants located in a foreign country? The United States is suffering from the worst economic and unemployment rates in years. We need to hire American workers in our manufacturing facilities in the United States. General Motors has been making plans to open a new manufacturing facility in Mexico. They propose to spend $500 million in developing the facility. Why is our government allowing this to happen? Our government owns about 61.2% of the stock in General Motors. How about using that $500 million to pay wages for building the plant in the United States and then paying American workers to build their products? We need the return of manufacturing to the country from Mexico, Canada, Asia and anywhere else that our goods and products are manufactured. Doesn't anyone in the business of producing goods remember "Made in the USA"?

It should make every American sick to the stomach every time they go into a Wal-Mart or similar discount store and the vast majority of the merchandise is made in some other country. When will the people wake up and start purchasing good products that are made in this country? I would think that America would be better off when the people realize that they can pay a couple of dollars more for a product and help everyone in this country instead of trying to save a dollar and help the rest of the world. Americans need to realize that charity and caring needs to start at home.

Notice no mention of the costs of illegal aliens to the rest of us. The social costs like health care, incarceration plus education are huge. In California it's half the budget deficit of the state. Anchor babies get welfare, around $700 a month and that does not include health care or education. That's just cash. There is another surreptitious cost - welfare costs for unskilled Americans whose jobs are taken by illegal workers because they work cheap and can't complain.

This debate about immigration may seem complex but it is actually probably pretty simple to most people. It seems like the Administration is tone deaf regarding how bad the job situation is across the country. Giving a general sweeping amnesty and actively defending millions of illegal aliens now when there are so many American citizens at risk of losing everything they have worked their whole lives for will be a losing position come election time. It is not about Republicans and Democrats.

It happens to be the Democrats who are currently defending what was obviously going to be an unsustainable status quo that has been in place for the last twenty years under Administrations of both parties. The Federal Government committed to address this issue when the last amnesty was given during the 1980's. We all remember. Given this the timing is real bad for Democrats regarding the Federal Government defending illegals on perceived principle versus the interests of most of the rest of the Americans. Most people have no problem with legal immigration because mostly everyone has someone in their family who is an immigrant but common sense would tell you if rule of law on this matter. Every other country on the planet enforces their immigration laws in the best interest of their citizens and most people know that because it is common sense. Basic logical thinking and economics would tell you the value of something, like citizenship is lessened for everyone if anyone can claim it by just taking it without following the rules and agreeing to buy in to a country's guiding principles and speak the language.

Anyone who thinks that "anchor babies" aren't a "racket" clearly does not live in a border state. Women make it across the river just in time to deliver their babies (at taxpayers' expense, of course) and then go home with their little anchors' citizenship papers in hand! This also makes the babies eligible for a host of government programs intended for real Americans, not accidental Americans, such as WIC, Medicaid, food stamps, free education, free meals at school, housing assistance, etc., if they stay here. Of course, the money is spent by the illegal alien parents, who also hope that having a kid who is a de facto citizen will help them avoid deportation. This loophole allows illegal aliens to steal US citizenship for their kids and we need to put a stop to it. The entire family needs to be sent home.

The mainstream media is not getting the accurate facts as well as the government's staff. That includes the New York Times, CNN, HLN, CBS, NBC, MSNBE and ABC. Go to California and the story you want is right in front of your eyes. It's impossible not to see if you visit an Orange County Hospital and check out the birth rates, even better check the census of California.

Here are some quotes for you from our media in LASD about English being a problem in our schools. We have over 250,000 students here with a English problem in our schools in Los Angeles and Orange County that can't speak English. How did we get in such a predicament? Why do we have children here from another country? How can you explain the English gap that is currently the problem? The federal government has been granting illegal citizens with a Free Pass. Have a child here and you get to enroll your children in our system which consists of: Welfare, Medical, Housing and Food assistance. Then we provide Citizenship for the children which they use to stay in the United States. We are obviously sending the wrong message to the people of Mexico.

They will pay someone to sneak them over the border and then stay at their relative's house and apply for papers for legalization. This has been going on for years and it's against the law.

Then they take real Americans jobs like in Medical, Manufacturing, Construction, Clerical, Gardening, Waste Management, Car washes etc. The farm laborers only account for 2% of the illegal workers that are taking the jobs from Americans. I believe we have given this country away to the citizens of Mexico with out a fight or representation of the people who fought for it. We have an epidemic of outrageous proportion.

The Department of Home Land Security in not making our country secure. There are about 20 million illegals through out the whole United States. An Illegal woman that was being released from prison after serving 25 years for murder, she said she was" Innocent" and now wants a pardon cause her children were born here and are now Legal American citizens. In other country's you can not be a citizen unless you are from that country. How could we let this happen when so many good Americans have fought for this right and died in the process and we give it away? Well the economics on this situation and it's direct affect on our own economy has got to be outrages and the taxpayers or real Americans are the one's that are paying the bill for them to come here and populate this country. Illegals should not be rewarded for breaking the law.

We must revise our immigration policies in order to have a country which can afford social and economic justice for its citizens, a country where citizens who are unemployed will find work. By ignoring illegal immigration we are contributing to the inability to provide United States citizens with the jobs, benefits, and protections they need. The government needs to provide money to the economy for training for and creating new jobs and new technologies.

Our economic system and tax system will never support open borders. One of the ways we are more likely to have a strong social service based environment in any state is to rewrite these laws. We must limit immigration and we must enforce immigration laws against illegal immigration. We could use Denmark as a model. Denmark has a strict immigration to citizenship policy which helps the country continue to guarantee education, housing, and medical benefits to all citizens as well as implement environmental policies for a sustained economy. It is quite difficult to become a citizen of Denmark yet it is one of the most liberal countries in the world in terms of civil rights and benefits.

It is just not true that "Liberal Democrat" equals "Open Borders" in terms of political policy. Some of us are more reality based than that. The people of Denmark have found out they must control immigration in order to have a society which is socially responsible. There are no anchor babies in Denmark. We should follow these examples and rewrite our citizen requirements.

We need new legislation to rewrite our immigration policies to realistically limit the number of people who can come into the country especially from Mexico and South America as this is where the majority of the illegal immigration originates. We should not grant amnesty to those who have broken the law. We cannot afford to any longer be a country which thinks it can provide jobs to everyone world wide when so many U.S. citizens are unemployed and underemployed and recent graduates cannot find work. It is a myth that immigrants do work no one else will do. Many are praying for entry level jobs at minimum pay and cannot get work. This is not about racial discrimination nor is it racial profiling although some will insist that it is. It is economic survival. If illegals stop filling jobs which should be given at a decent minimum wage American citizens will fill those slots.

It is right to seek out employers who hire illegal immigrants and level heavy fines against them. Insist on fair wages and working conditions. Deport illegal workers and the undocumented. Send a new message to those who want to come here and do cheap labor and who undercut the minimum wage. Send a message that times have changed

It appears that United States has requirements for legal immigrants that it objects to for illegal immigrants. Legal immigrants have said they have to carry proof of their status; they have to learn English, and they have to pass a test on the Constitution. The effect of the current federal policy is dissemination against legal immigrants.

At the same time, we need to strictly enforce our laws against hiring illegal aliens, with harsh fines for employers for a first offense, and jail time and loss of business license for repeat offenders. Make every employer, even for day labor, check the legality of his employees through a national data base, and require the payment of income taxes. I would suggest not deducting SS, since they would not be eligible to receive it. This would eliminate the advantage of using cheap labor and greatly decrease the availability of work for illegal aliens. We can make it clear to these people that if they can't be bothered to come legally, they are unwelcome and need to go back home.

According to the Bureau of the Census, the population of the U.S. is about to explode from 300 million a few years ago to nearly 400 million in only 40 more years -- and most of that will be due to illegal immigration. The two major components driving the population growth are fertility (births) and net immigration. After 2011, the number of births each year would exceed the highest annual number of births ever achieved in the United States. Almost one-third of the current population growth is caused by illegal immigration.

Of the U.S. population of nearly 400 million in 2050, nearly 1 in 4 (23 percent) will be Hispanic, mostly from Mexico. That's nearly 100 million residents of the United States who have been taught that the United States forcefully and unfairly took from them one half their former countries?

The only reason Arizona passed SB-1080 is that the federal government has shown it is incapable or unwilling to control illegal immigration. We have had several amnesties, but the illegals just keep coming. This is bad for population control, for low income workers who have to compete with illegals, for our budget problems, and it contributes to a feeling that laws don't matter. I hope we can get rid of the anchor baby concept. Other countries don't use it. Other countries have interior enforcement where people can be asked for their papers.

We have a nation that is several times as large as most other countries, many thousands of miles of borders and coastlines and several millions of visa bearing visitors every year. Unless we were to expand the INS or ICE there is no way that federal enforcement alone could ever effectively control criminal immigration. Interestingly other federal agencies routinely solve this problem by asking local police to look for and detain specific persons or certain kinds of criminals. The fact that so many in power in this country oppose this same common sense cooperation in regard to immigration makes it very obvious that this country's elites just do not want our immigration laws enforced. This would not be much of a moral or legal problem if the majority of Americans did not want these laws enforced, but continual polls indicate that approximately 80% of Americans do. This means that both political parties think it appropriate to defy the popular will in this supposed democratic country. This increasing contempt for the common person in our country in regard to so many issues is a much bigger problem than that of immigration law enforcement alone.

The Federal Government is demonstrating that they are totally inept and uninterested in defending our borders. In typical fashion they demonstrate that they cannot perform any task efficiently. Janet Napolitano is inept and not interested in doing the job. She should be removed. The Anchor Baby policy is absurd, it should be eliminated.

President Obama is like his predecessors, not interested. He states that "we cannot deport 20 million illegals" they found a way to get here, let them find their way home. It would cost a lot less to give each one a plane ticket than support them.

The Constitution is a contract between the States, and the United States government. The States gave to the U.S. government their right to secure their borders. Under the Constitution, the U.S. government agreed to do that for them. Also, the U.S government agreed to remove all illegal immigrants from the States if any get across the border. The court did not take into account the fact that the U.S. is not performing its duty to secure the border, nor to remove illegal immigrants from the States. Since the U.S. government is in violation of the contract between the States and the U.S., and then the States under contract law have every right, while the U.S. refuses to secure the border and remove illegals, to take on their sovereign powers and do it themselves.

The government's rights are only secured to it, if it is abiding by the contract it has with Arizona and the other States, and it clearly is not. The millions of illegals in the U.S. make that abundantly clear, not even taking in the fact that the U.S. knows of millions of illegals in our schools whom the U.S. is making no attempt to remove from the county. Not only does the U.S. refuse to perform its job of securing the borders and removing illegals, they federal government demands that the States spend their revenues to provide these illegals with educations, medical care, and due process rights at a great cost to the States. In California, four hospitals have closed their doors, gone bankrupt because of the cost of providing care to illegals. Further, the State reports that another fourteen hospitals in California are in danger of closing their doors as well because of this unfunded mandate from the Federal government, because the U.S. signed treaties guaranteeing foreign nationals human rights while in the United States. If these hospitals close their doors as well, over 2.5 million Californians will be without local hospital services.

Made in the USA

CHAPTER TWENTY

The Environmentalists Situation

According to the latest statistics from the United States International Trade Commission, United States imports of crude oil amounted to $60.4 billion for the first 4 months of 2010. That figure represents a 65.4% increase over the $36.5 billion that America spent on crude petroleum imports from January to April 2009. If that pace continues, total crude oil imports will cost an estimated $181 billion for 2010 which would be America's second highest expenditure on imported crude over the past 10 years. The total oil bill for 2010 will have been exceeded only by the $259.3 billion bill spent on imported crude oil during 2008.

These crude oil purchases would not be required if we developed the natural resources that are in our own country. How can we Americans be so stupid as to let one group of citizens have so much control over our country? The number of jobs that would be created would include: trucking, construction, engineering, housing, service, accommodations, refining, manufacturing, and many others to support the exploration industry. When the government starts to produce its own crude to eliminate the need for imported oil we will be able to install a reasonable tax increase per gallon of 10 cents and we will generate $17.922 billion in revenue. Take the 4,267,110,000 barrels of crude oil during 2009 times the 42 gallons per barrel and the tax it at 10 cents a gallon. When you figure that the average American uses 100 gallons per month the cost per individual is only $10.00. I would rather pay the extra few dollars and help get my country back to respectability and eliminate the deficits. That sure would be a lot better than sending $181 billion to the foreign countries around the world.

That would be in addition to the amount saved by not having to purchase crude oil from the Middle East and other countries. A great start to create a balanced budget. That would be a major improvement to our economic system and our balance of trade deficit.

Further benefits to the United States economy would be the natural gas that is captured during the process of extracting the crude oil. The United States utilizes 3,981 billion cubic feet of natural gas per day. The average cost per 1,000 cubic feet of natural gas was $7.00 in 2008. You can figure out how much money we are wasting by not producing our own natural gas. When this amount of natural gas is produced from our natural resources it will produce $1.453 billion in tax to the government.

The Congress needs to take control of our country and initiate legislation that will open up the exploration into all parts of the United States. The country just can not afford to waste our resources to save a few trees. We can build additional sections of our beautiful parks after the exploration has been completed. This will provide more usable recreation areas instead of just vast wildernesses.

Technology Helps Reduce Drilling's "Footprint"

Exploring and drilling for natural gas will always have some impact on land and marine habitats. But new technologies have greatly reduced the number and size of areas disturbed by drilling, sometimes called "footprints." Plus, the use of horizontal and directional drilling makes it possible for a single well to produce gas from much bigger areas than in the past.

Natural gas pipelines and storage facilities have a good safety record. This is important because when natural gas leaks it can cause explosions. Since raw natural gas has no odor, natural gas companies add a smelly substance to it so that people will know if there is a leak. If you have a natural gas stove, you may have smelled this "rotten egg" smell of natural gas when the pilot light has gone out.

What can be done to work with environmental groups so that we can develop the natural resources of the United States? When is the government going to start to realize that the environmentalists are causing major problems and massive deficits? The United States has huge quantities of natural resources within the borders of this country. We need to relax the regulations so that they can be utilized. What good are all these resources if we do not use them for the good of the entire nation? The time has come to start drilling for crude oil and natural gas in the Rocky Mountain Regions and the wilderness areas of Alaska. There are credible reports that there are enough resources in these regions to satisfy the needs of the United States for the next 30 to 40 years. The price of foreign oil will go to about $20.00 per barrel since there will not be any demand from the United States. Wake up America.

There needs to be legislation passed that will commence the exploration and production of the vast amounts of natural resources that are within our country. There can be safe guards implemented that will protect our environment. We can not afford to keep depending upon foreign countries to provide us with our petroleum requirements especially when we can be doing it. The policy of importing our petroleum products is creating a huge trade deficit and transferring the wealth of our great nation to the Middle East. I do not want to be dependent upon that area of the world.

The future tax revenues from the production of our own petroleum products will provide the United States with a huge surplus every year and the budget will always be in balance. The deficit spending will be gone and the trillions of accumulated deficit can be paid off. This can be done with our own resources and eliminate the debt of our children and their children.

The environmentalists need to take their heads out of the sand that they are desperately trying to protect. Why is it so hard for them to see that to save a tree might mean that they actually are going to be the largest contributor in destroying the United States of America? I agree that America is the most beautiful place on earth. We do not have to destroy that beauty to protect our nation from being destroyed by the massive deficits. If we are not careful we will not have to worry about our environment because we won't own our country any more. That would be the worst thing that could ever happen to America and we can not let that happen.

The potential revenue from exploring the Rocky Mountain Region and the Alaskan wilderness would be enough to solve our deficit problems for the next 30 years. The states in those regions would be financially sound and capital would be freed up to benefit other states as well. We just can not afford to sit on these resources and let the United States struggle with our deficits and economy. In addition, by opening up these areas we will create substantial employment not only in the exploration industry but others as well. It is just the right thing to do and the time is now.

There are billions of barrels of crude oil in the regions that would provide massive amounts of income for the United States. For example if 10 billion barrels of crude are located in the region it could generate $100 billion in revenues to the government by taxing it at $10.00 per barrel. That would sure beat paying the Middle East $75.00 per barrel for crude.

It is past the time to be "Politically Correct" and propose the proper legislation in Congress and start thinking about what is good for all of the people. We do not need to placate the environmental segment of our population at the sacrifice of the rest of the citizens and the country. Do this legislation now.

The government could raise several billion dollars by taking bids from the oil companies to drill and recover these vast amounts of reserves. The government will only be allowed to take bids from American companies that are paying their income taxes. Protection and clean-up clauses could be placed in all the contract bids so that the environment will be left in great shape.

With all the screaming by the environmentalists about drilling in these areas how about the massive wind farms that are springing up all over the country? These are ugly, noisy and are killing the avian that migrate every year. Have any of you ever driven into Oakland, California in the evening on Highway 5 and heard the weird sounds. It is like going into a Halloween three movie set. These wind farms are creating a much larger eye sore that any drilling activity will cause.

The environmental activists are damaging the future of the United States instead of protecting our future. This is just one issue that they need to get over and save America.

Another aspect of the exploration is the amount of income tax that would be generated and the American companies would be paid the $372,646 billion instead of sending it to the foreign countries. If the production companies return a 15% net operating profit that they have to pay income tax on it will generate $19.565 billion. The production companies could pay to their employees 20% of the revenue to cover expenses which would generate $74.529 billion that would go directly into the economy. The social security and Medicare tax deductions along would generate an additional $11.179 billion in tax revenue for the government. We are not even taking into consideration the capital expenditures and the benefits to the local economies. This part of the equation will generate a total of $30.744 billion in revenue to the federal government.

Fuel taxes in the United States vary by state. For the first quarter of 2009, the mean state gasoline tax is 27.2 cents per US gallon, plus 18.4 cents per US gallon federal tax making the total 45.6 cents per US gallon. For diesel, the mean state tax is 26.6 cents per US gallon plus an additional 24.4 cents per US gallon federal tax making the total 50.8 cents US per gallon. There are also a few states that charge sales tax on top of the excise taxes and the retail price.

I know that the figures do not add up. The correct total should be $2,565 billion from the numbers that they included in the budget. Maybe this is some kind of new math. Oh well, what's a couple of billion? These figures are from page 151 of the federal budget.

The Presidents proposed federal budget for 2011 shows the following items as receipts for the federal government.

Receipts:	Amount in billions:
Individual Income Taxes	$1,121
Corporate Income Taxes	297
Social Security Payroll Taxes	674
Medicare Payroll Taxes	192

Unemployment Insurance	60
Other Retirement	8
Excise Taxes	74
Estate and Gift Taxes	25
Customs Duties	27
Earnings Federal Reserve System	79
Allowance for Jobs Incentives	(25)
Allowance for Health Reform	16
Other Miscellaneous Receipts	17
Total Receipts	$2,567

Since the tax receipts from petroleum products do not show up in the federal budget it makes one wonder just where they show up and who is accounting for them? When we consider that the United States uses 4,271,110,000 barrels of crude oil per year. Each barrel produces 42 gallons of gasoline. That would be 179,386,620,000 gallons of gasoline. The federal government is charging the consumers of the gasoline 18.4 cents per gallon. The revenue could be in the range of $3.3 trillion. I would like to know where these funds are accounted for and who is making the decisions on how this money is allocated? This is almost as much as the entire federal budget. Something smells a little fishy here.

In the United States, the fuel tax receipts are often dedicated or hypothecated to transportation projects so that the fuel tax is considered by many a user fee. In other countries, the fuel tax is a source of general revenue. If these are user fees they should be for the improvement of our roads, bridges and other federal projects that are for the transportation sector of our economy. Then I must ask why did the government $787 billion stimulus need to be primarily for road, rail and airport improvements?

CHAPTER TWENTY ONE

The Poor Getting Poorer

Recent articles have shown that the poor class of citizens just keeps growing and getting poorer due to the legislation that has been passed by the federal government.

One of the most glaring aspects of the poor is the problems caused by having 20 million illegals in the country that are generally in the lower level of income or in the poverty level. It's not that hard to understand. Most Americans don't want the wholesale importation of low skilled migrants who lower wages on jobs, take social services they don't pay into and fail to learn fluent English.

We're sick and tired of being used as a dumping ground for Mexico, Central America and South America's excess population woes. Protesting such idiotic policies is understandable self interest rather than bigotry.

Recent articles in the news had a story about the devastating challenges faced by the shrinking American middle class - about the richest getting richer, the poor poorer, and the middle class disappearing. The real American taxpayers - the middle class paid Goldman Sachs, AIG - and all the rest. We got royally screwed even as these companies paid bonuses and salaries that should have been used instead of taxpayer money.

Unfortunately it is the rules fault. As the rules, regulations, techniques have been decades in the creation both parties feed at the trough of greed, but even more perniciously, the richest - corporate and individual alike have been allowed to control, influence, misdirect, and redirect American policy to their benefit for decades. As a perfect illustration of the pernicious influence of corporations, simply consider Goldman Sachs's direct path through highest level government posts, to subtly direct policies to support their personal economic beliefs. The government regularly appoints Goldman Sachs's executives and then we're surprised when those policy decisions benefit Goldman Sachs. Go figure? Continuously, while we weren't paying attention, understanding the details, the richest, individual and corporate alike are now in a position where what's good for Goldman Sachs's is good for the United States regardless of wider and more profound implications.

We recommend that you cut up your Chase credit card, Withdraw all funds from Goldman Sachs brokerage account, cancel your AIG insurance and refinance your Wells Fargo mortgage with your local savings & loan. The only way to get the bankers attention is to attack their profits. 61 Senators voted against to big to fail so that if we have another problem United States citizens will again be forced to bail the banks out. As long as big money is involved, average citizens will not change the vote of either party. Put your money where your mouth is and hit them in their wallet. It is the only real way to affect change.

First, the story is about AIG and its investment arm, AIG Auto was actually making money for the company and was sold off to Farmers Insurance during the restructure as a profitable business. Now, do we understand way AIG was so important to the Fed? Here's why: The pension funds for Congress and the Senate are heavily vested in AIG. Do you understand now? These guys in Washington watched the stock market crash to the ground and picked the three largest investment firms to bail out so they could keep from losing their pensions while you were losing ours. This wasn't a Democrat or Republican thing. It was complete collusion of self interest by the whole group.

Bailouts, no matter the reasoning, are a terrible thing in a capitalist economic system. Businesses fail everyday. It doesn't matter if you employ one person or tens of thousands, if your company if failing then so be it. It is not the responsibility of the citizens of the United States to loan you money. If your creditors don't loan you the money there's probably a pretty good reason. When we apply and get turned down for loans there's a reason. Insolvency is insolvency. If you can't afford to repay a loan then you are denied. All these bail out companies should have folded or sold to the highest bidder for their assets. All this bailout stuff did was covering the rears of a few and cost the rest of us a trillion dollars. I don't see the government paying us the interest they are collecting from these companies. So, Washington saves their pension and collects the interest of the money we loaned them. We got jerked on both ends of this bailout.

CHAPTER TWENTY TWO

The Real Estate Market

Given the importance of the housing market to the nation's balance sheet, it's no surprise that many observers are looking for any evidence that prices on family homes have finally bottomed out. For those watchers, November had a bit of good news: The National Association of Realtors reported that its index of sales agreements for previously occupied homes rose 10.4 % in October 2010.

But that positive statistic must be placed in a longer-term context of declining prices, bulging inventories of unsold homes and ongoing legal improprieties in the nation's foreclosure machinery. And against that background, the National Association of Realtors news doesn't feel all that impressive.

The rise in sales agreements is also clouded by reports that new-home sales fell 8.1% in October to a seasonally adjusted annual pace of only 283,000, a near-record low, while existing-home sales declined 2.2% to an annual rate of about 4 million. In the third quarter, home sales tumbled 25% to a 4.16 million seasonally adjusted annual pace from the previous three months, a rate that was 21% below the 5.28 million clip of 2009's third quarter.

Some real estate analysts foresee another three years of price declines as the massive inventory of underwater and foreclosed homes is slowly sold off, and we need look no further than the basics of supply and demand to understand why: Analysts estimate that as many as 12 million more properties will be put up for sale over the next few years. If about 4 million homes are sold annually, then it would take three years to clear the backlog.

The so-called "shadow inventory" of unsold homes -- bank-owned properties that are being held out of the market by lenders -- is also rising. The banks have sold around 700,000 homes in foreclosures during the past nine months that is down 25% from last year's sales. Analysts from Morgan Stanley estimate that the number of bank-owned and foreclosure-bound homes that have yet to hit the market is close to 8 million.

In light of this imbalance between supply and demand, some real estate observers expect house prices to fall another 8% to 10% from the current levels.

Nearly one-quarter of all United States homeowners with a mortgage -- 11 million borrowers -- owed more than their homes were worth as of June 30, 2010, according to real estate analysts. Another 2.4 million borrowers had less than 5% equity in their houses and would likely lose money on a sale after paying broker fees and closing costs.

Given the millions of homes in the foreclosure pipeline it is little wonder that prices are falling in most markets. Demand for foreclosed properties fell off a cliff in the third quarter, providing more evidence that housing appears to entering a second leg down after prices and sales recovered in 2009 and early 2010.

According to the Federal Reserve's most recent Flow of Funds Report, homeowners' equity is down about $6 trillion from the 2006 top in real estate prices. While the recovery in home valuations boosted homeowners' equity from a low of $6 trillion up to $7 trillion, homeowners' equity as a percentage of home values is still down from a high near 60% to 40%. Since one-third of American homes are owned free and clear, most of that equity resides in homes that are unencumbered by mortgages.

Home mortgage debt has slipped modestly from $10.5 trillion to $10.15

trillion, largely as a result of lenders' write-downs in short sales -- where homes are sold for less than the mortgage owed and the bank accepts the loss -- and foreclosure auctions.

So, while the recent recovery in sales and prices has lifted homeowners' equity somewhat, households have still lost $6 trillion in equity, and one-quarter have no equity at all and owe more on their mortgages than their homes are worth. Household mortgage debt is still close to the levels reached at the peak of the housing bubble.

Though lenders insist they have restarted foreclosure proceedings with more careful attention to due process, a host of legal actions are calling that claim into question.

In one recent case, U.S. Bankruptcy Court Judge Judith H. Wizmur rejected a foreclosure claim on the home of John T. Kemp of New Jersey, ruling that his mortgage company had failed to deliver the note to the trustee as required when it sold the mortgage. That may leave the new trustee, Bank of New York Mellon, with no standing to foreclose, and the ruling casts doubt on the legality of many, many other foreclosures.

Other legal battles have erupted over short sales as the primary mortgage holders have been stymied by lenders holding second mortgages who refuse to sign off on sales that give them little of the proceeds.

Meanwhile, real estate attorneys are poring over thousands of records, scanning for serious errors which could negate foreclosure claims by lenders, while holders of mortgage-backed securities are pushing banks to buy back improperly transferred mortgages.

The market of possible buyers has shrunk as well. As the Federal Housing Administration has guaranteed more mortgages in recent years, the default rate on FHA loans has skyrocketed. In an attempt to stem this rising tide of foreclosures, lenders have raised their minimum credit score on FHA-insured loans to 640 from 620. That will exclude about 6 million people from the pool of potential homebuyers, according to FICO, which created the formula for the ratings.

With over 9% of prime mortgages now in default, it's especially troubling to industry observers that the loan modification programs designed to save households from future defaults are experiencing re-default rates of 50%, meaning half of the households that receive mortgage modifications end up defaulting again within a year.

Add all these factors up, and it seems likely that the housing market will remain unsettled in for several more years.

What some of our citizens think about the current housing market and the chances of early recovery?

Folks just got back from a fact finding trip on home purchases in Florida and Nevada. The inventory of homes on sale is glutted beyond belief. Any home in Florida bought in Citrus, Marion, or Brevard counties over $40,000 is money you'll never get back, at least for the next 15 years. Las Vegas is glutted with huge mansions with pools and huge lots, all bank owned, all around $110,000, and no takers at all. Our "jobless" recovery, with a real unemployment rate at about 18-20%, means that there is no demand in a glutted home market. Prices can only go down. You have mortgage rates at historic lows but without jobs and a pessimistic future, who thinks about buying a home? The Federal Reserve printing more money will only create an eventual deflation, where homes prices will continue to tumble. Do not buy now be patient, a nice home in Florida or Nevada will be available for $20,000.

Fannie Mae and Freddie Mac originally had very strict eligibility requirements for the types of mortgages they would purchase. When they were the only one buying up mortgages, retail banks and non-bank lenders were pretty much limited to offering plain vanilla 30 year fixed conforming mortgages. When Wall Street went directly to the lenders and said "we will buy anything Fannie Mae and Freddie Mac won't", it opened up the door to more exotic mortgages. Since they carried extra risk, they paid a higher interest rate. That allowed Wall Street to offer higher yields on its Mortgage Backed Securities than Fannie Mae and Freddie Mac. In response, Fannie Mae and Freddie Mac expanded the spectrum of the types of mortgages they would buy. They did so with the tacit approval of most people in congress, because it did keep rates lower than they would have been otherwise, and it allowed minorities and the poor to buy homes they otherwise could not have afforded. The reason

Fannie Mae and Freddie Mac expanded into the sub-prime market was to compete with Wall Street. Until about 2003, they were the only entity that was securitizing mortgages in any meaningful quantity. Around that time, Wall Street realized that it could bypass Fannie Mae and Freddie Mac and securitize them directly, using SIVs, and CDO structures. Wall Street doesn't make mortgages, retail banks and non-bank lenders like Countrywide do. Wall Street buys those mortgages and then packages them. Barney Frank has consistently opposed any measure to reform Fannie Mae and Freddie Mac. In 2003, the Bush Administration proposed legislation to reform the two, Frank killed it in committee. In 2005, the Bush Administration tried again, Frank again killed it in committee. He led a united Democratic opposition, which found a single Republican in 1 instance, and 2 Republicans in the second to kill the bill. Is he solely to blame, no, of course not. However, my comment was in response to someone asking why people are blaming the Democrats. My response was that Democrats opposed any reform of Fannie Mae and Freddie Mac because it would interfere with their social mission of encouraging home ownership. These are the facts. Actually, the Bush Administration did propose legislation to limit the types of exotic mortgages that Fannie Mae and Freddie Mac could purchase. It was a function of economic reality. Fannie Mae and Freddie Mac's core mission is to facilitate the mortgage market. It has become an ancillary mission to encourage home ownership. At the height of the bubble, there were key Democrats (namely Barney Frank) pushing them to move into these profitable new types of mortgages, in order to generate more cash to fund that ancillary mission.

Politicians who say we need more regulation almost never mean regulation in the sense of impartially enforcing explicit rules, such as the accounting rules that Fannie Mae was violating to cover up its own risks. They mean regulation with arbitrary powers, such as those under the Community Reinvestment Act, which enable regulators to carry out the agendas that politicians give them. When Congressman Jim Leach tried to get stronger regulation of Fannie Mae and Freddie Mac back in 1992, and when President George W. Bush did so in 2004, Barney Frank opposed them. A reining in of Fannie Mae and Freddie Mac would be a reining in of Barney Frank's power.

You bet the sale of bank owned (REO) properties is down. The banks acquire all these homes through foreclosure. And then just let the properties sit and fall in to such disrepair, that it would cost a potential buyer of a foreclosed property more in repairs, and then the foreclosed home is worth. This policy puts a potential home buyer of a foreclosed home in a very high risk/shaky financial position, due to the cost of repairs needed on the home. The initial purchase price of a foreclosed property may seem like a good buy. However, the cost of repairs to the home will most likely become a financial nightmare for the majority of buyers. Then there is the problem of getting title insurance. With all the problems with the mortgage documents people are not going to take a chance purchasing one of these homes.

I HAVE A FRIEND WHOM OWNS A PRIVATE MORTGAGE FUNDING COMPANY,BASICALLY HE POOLS INVESTORS TOGETHER THAT WOULD NORMALLY PUT THEIR CASH IN THE BANKS AND GET A SAFE RETURN ON THEIR FUNDS,HOWEVER SINCE BANKS ARE THE WRONG PLACE TO PUT ANYTHING NOWADAYS WHAT HE DOES IS BASICALLY POOL THE FUNDS TOGETHER AND LEND OUT TO THOSE usually to the wealthy yes I said it to the wealthy most people think the rich have money laying all over the place but that is not the case usually it is on paper tied up for some length of time .IN UNIQUE SIUATIONS they need short term loans normally stuff banks even when they were strong would not touch . ,YES THERE ARE RISK BUT THE RATE OF RETURN IS MUCH HIGHER THAN ANYTHING OUT THERE ALSO HE KEEPS ALL INVESTMENTS CLOSE TO HOME WITHIN THE STATE THUS LOTS OF HOMEWORK CAN BE DONE PRIOR TO CLOSING A DEAL. Anyways this is the same guy that told me a few years back that oil would be going for over $112.00 a barrel. I remember this because I told several so they thought at the time they were savvy investors and they all laughed and said your boy don't know what he is talking about. Never in our life time would we see the price of oil go that high. Well as we all know it went that high and then some. So now they all want to know what my friend says about the housing market. Well we have not spoken in over six months but back then that was one of the questions I did ask him at that time he did say if your thinking of buying now with all the bank owned inventory on the market and the huge price decline from the hay days, don't at least till after 2014 then come talk to me. Back then he told me as a friend I'm telling you this there is way too much inventory and way too much inventory being held back by the banks and way too many homes yet underwater which have yet to be taken back by the banks and then placed on the market. Well from what I have seen this guy did not get where he is today being stupid making stupid choices. Today he is doing fine as I am as well but only due to the fact that I listened and took his advice. And believe it or not I own a construction company yes we are not making the type of profits we were making years back but we are paying the bills and living comfortable. In an industry which has in most cases ceased to exist.

Our bank told us they don't want our home back. My husband lost his job of almost 30 years last year and now it's getting harder and harder to make that monthly payment. The bank won't help us but even though they say they don't want our home back, they'll take it once they find out we can't pay for it anymore. They can have it back. But they aren't getting anything that we have put into it over the last 10 years. That means this house would be nothing but a shell. We've done everything to our home! It's not fair that the banks will kick people out of their home but then turn around and sell that same home for a fraction of what the original owner paid. How moronic is this system? They are ruining families and losing money in the long run anyhow so why not just allow the people to remain in their homes and adjust their mortgage to what the home would sell for today? Nope, they are rat bastards that don't give a damn! We didn't work all these years to be thrown out of our home! It's bad enough the company my husband worked for was allowed to cut their older, more higher paid employees! The whole thing stinks! We're middle aged grandparents that have owned 3 homes, raised our kids and should be getting ready to retire. Now we have to scramble for jobs that aren't available to people like us because the market is flooded with people like us.

We had much lower unemployment under President Bush; but Ms. Pelosi said it was too high - now she is silent when unemployment is above 9.8% - where's the ranting now? Housing will not recover for at least 6 years - or until Mr. Obama is out of office. Those under foreclosure according to a person I know in the real estate business can avoid paying their mortgages but rent out their residences and pocket the rent. Socialism has never worked in any country where it has been tried - if America gets back to what we stand for - hard work; minimal government interference, and savings for the future; plus a rejection of products made in China (which is just about everything) then we will start a dynamic recovery. Pray for this country every day.

I'm a retired savings and loan/banking person. We have another 5 to 8 years of trouble remaining in the housing industry. What are people thinking about values in their homes when they go to sell, listing it at 2007 levels and then the property doesn't appraise anywhere near that level? Take a minimum 25% haircut on what you think your house is worth and you'll sell it, folks. Otherwise...wait another 5-8 years.

Bernanke admitted in his 60 Minutes interview that he did not see the panic of 2008 coming. His excuse was that the Fed didn't have oversight of AIG or Lehman Brothers, and if the Fed had more powers they would have seen the crisis coming. There are many Austrian economists, including those who co-founded and are associated with NIA, who did see the panic of 2008 coming. Every Austrian economist who predicted the panic of 2008 now believes that massive inflation is in our future. It doesn't make sense for Americans to trust Bernanke about inflation when he was wrong about the housing bubble and just about everything else. Bernanke went on to say that the reason the U.S. has the largest income disparity gap out of any country in the world is because of "educational differences". Bernanke claims that unemployment for Americans with college degrees is only 5%, compared to 10% unemployment for Americans with just a high school education. The truth is the reason for our income disparity gap is inflation. When the Fed prints money, it steals from the incomes and savings of the poor and middle-class and transfers this wealth to those on Wall Street who have access to the Fed's cheap and easy money. It has nothing to do with education. In fact, because of Bernanke making it so easy for college students to get student loans, the U.S. has a college tuition inflation crisis. College tuitions now cost 60% of the median U.S. income, triple the rate of 20% which held strong from 1950 to 1980. Americans today who have college degrees are now worst off, because they are deeply into debt. The only reason their rate of unemployment is lower than those without college degrees is because those with college degrees are more determined to find jobs. If you ask any college graduate who has a job if their college degree helped them become employed, NIA believes the overwhelming majority of college graduates will tell you no. Bernanke says that he is "trying to achieve balance" and "will not allow inflation to rise above 2%". He says the Fed can "raise interest rates in 15 minutes if we have to" and the

Fed will have "no problem raising rates, tightening monetary policy, and reducing inflation when the time is appropriate".

The Socialists want to redistribute the wealth but exactly the opposite is happening. Now that middle class and poor people are losing their homes to foreclosure, those of us who have money are buying them up and renting them back to them. Most recent sales prices of homes here in Arizona provide investors with about a 20% to 30% return on investment with a 20% down payment. They believe the socialist propaganda and get screwed every time. Hard work and savings is the answer not Obama's plan to redistribute wealth.

There is the problem. You have fallen for the lies from the left. They tell the public what you say they want to give to the poor and take from the rich. Not the case they seek to increase more poverty to increase power. Soon they will seek absolute power and take the remaining wealth for themselves a doctorial single party ruling class. Look how far they have convinced the so called Republicans in office to their ends. Yep that's right they too will throw away values for wealth and power.

Yeah, it is all Barney Frank and Chris Dodd because they wanted to make home ownership easier. This after Bush wanted an ownership society as early as 2004. No one ordered bankers to securitize mortgages, or lower credit requirements, or not do due diligence in checking out applicants. Not all banks failed in this regard, only the greedy ones. You can also blame a GOP Congress for overturning Glass-Stiegel in the late '90's, allowing commercial banks and investment banks to merge. At the time it was done, there was a great championing of what this new assist to the financial industry and the efficiency of banking this would be. For years it worked just fine and a lot of people made money. The bigger problem was that people were using their home equity as a piggy bank and buying, buying, buying, which is what kept the economy afloat. Also glad to see your head is stuck in the past, which is where conservatives would rather be. Pretty soon you'll at least have to come into this decade.

How much lower can interest rates be lowered? Let the banks that foreclose and take the loss of on a un-sold home that gets condemned and looses all possibility of recovering any value sink in. They will get motivated and prices will go down until the market agrees to take it of their hands. If the banks are to stupid to save as much value as possible then let them go under. See this is what happens when the banks know they will be bailed out. The bail outs did just the opposite of what the Federal Reserve morons are saying it did. Truth is they don't care they have bigger plans for America. They aren't pretty plans.

And the only thing that will help begin to turn it around is: people need to have jobs and regain confidence in the direction that the country is headed. And there is far too much uncertainty in the economy with the current administration. I personally know some wealthy investors who recently told me that they are sitting on wads of cash. But they refuse to invest in expanding or hiring because they are afraid of how the administration will punish them through higher taxes. They are already faced with higher health care costs thanks to Obamacare.

It is illustrative that our own president does not know what our system of government is; Obama repeatedly refers to the U.S. as a democracy, when in fact we have a representative republic! If you are looking for an impeachable offense, consider this: the "stimulus" package of approx. $800,000,000,000.00 amounted to a transfer of spending authority from the House of Representatives to the executive branch of government. Such a transfer is NOT constitutionally allowable, and should be the basis of impeachment of all members of congress who voted for this, as well as the president.

SOME HOMEOWNERS COMMENTS ON THE STATE OF THE HOUSING MARKET

It is tough right now to consider buying or even selling. People are not doing either. There is uncertainty about our jobs and home value. I would love to sell my home and move to another area. I don't even bother with it, I know I won't get enough selling the house as I should with the way things are right now. And then I know if I try to buy another home it will be over-priced than what it should be. Stuck in the middle and will just have to wait it out.

Nobody is safe in their jobs anymore. We thought we were secure until my husband lost his job of almost 30 years last year. Now everything has been a struggle. There aren't any jobs out there for middle aged factory workers and even worse, it seems that everyone wants some kind of a degree and years experience. We have the years of experience but back in our day we never had the chance to get a degree and really didn't need it until now. But now is too late. We don't have the money for schooling, we're grandparents that should be retiring but now we have to scramble for crap jobs that are all taken because the market is flooded with people just like us. Our bank doesn't want to work with us in saving our home but yet they claim they don't want it back. We shouldn't have to start looking for someplace to live! We've owned 3 homes with this bank over the last 24 years and have never had a late payment. They have the nerve not to work with us when we've been good loyal customers for all these years. They'll take our home and turn around and sell it for a fraction of its price to someone else but they won't just allow us to re mortgage it for what it's worth today. Something is terribly wrong here.

In the Washington, DC area, real-estate values are improving... especially on high-end homes. Guess why? Guess who is busy spending taxpayers' hard-earned money on overpaid bureaucrats? Did you know that a two-income family of government employees might easily earn a salary of $250,000 and on top of those earnings, are often already receiving pensions from other government jobs from which they've retired, boosting their income up to $300,000 or $400,000 or more? Remember when government jobs weren't lucrative, but at least they were steady work? Well, now they're steady (to the point where you can't even fire incompetent workers), and they're overpaid, and they receive benefits and pension plans the likes of which nobody in the private sector will ever see. Wonder why our nation is so far in debt? Did your congress critter vote himself another raise, too, in addition to boosting budgets for all those unionized government employees? Had enough yet? Or do you want more of the same, lame, establishment politicians (both Democrats and Republicans) who keep screwing you over to finance a wealthy free-for-all for the elites? Wake up, America, the party is over.

I wouldn't buy a house right now even if we could afford to. I'd be too afraid I'd wake up one morning and find we were being foreclosed on for no reason by some bank (which I had never dealt with before) that claimed to own my mortgage but couldn't find the deed, hadn't read the paperwork, and wouldn't sit down with us and try to straighten things out.

October 3, 2010 the news media reported that the already fragile United States financial firms will be facing thousands of lawsuits and probably major fines after the major mortgage lending institutes revealed that they improperly handled tens of thousands of home foreclosure documents that they were responsible for certifying.

The mortgage lenders that were involved in the mishandling of foreclosure documents were Bank of America, J.P. Morgan and GMAC have admitted that they were not using the proper procedures in processing foreclosures. These practices were happening across the country. The Attorney Generals of the states involved are already preparing to file lawsuits against the firms.

The foreclosure business started with the economic downturn in late 2008. The industry has grown to a huge industry since the start of the economic downturn that Americans have faced. Americans have incurred massive debts, with the number of mortgage defaults soaring from an annual average of one percent before 2008 to 10 percent today. During 2010 there will be more than three million homes that are lost to foreclosure with the prediction that over 60% of those foreclosures will have serious problems with their documents. This is just another example of the shoddy practices that the real estate industry was practicing in the years leading up to the real estate market crash.

The document problem is not going to give much relief to the majority of the homeowners but it is going to delay the foreclosure of a huge number of properties for years to come. The real estate market is going to be depressed for years until this mess is resolved. The greed and sloppiness of the lending institutes created this problem by not hiring enough staff to properly handle the foreclosure documents. Hopefully this will result in these companies receiving major fines and disciplinary actions.

These lenders are going to be facing substantial lawsuits from the homeowners that have proven that there were serious flaws in their documentation. The good part is that these homeowners are going to be in a positive position to force a better compromise on their mortgage. There is a potential for class action liability in the United States for billions and billions of dollars on behalf of homeowners who lost their homes in proceedings where lenders used these kinds of phony documents.

This is not going to help the real estate market since the glut of foreclosed homes in going to remain for years to come. The value of homes will remain at unrealistic levels until the foreclosure all of the foreclosures are finally on the market. That is going to take years.

The mortgage business is a major problem in the United States and solving the problem is not going to be easy. It is going to take a lot of patience and fortitude be every party involved. We are not going to even try and compute how this will affect the budget. We will however try and present some ideas that might help with the solution.

The problems started when banks and other financial institutions were forced by government to give a home credit to buyers who can not qualify for a loan, the qualification requirements were ignored. All the prospective home buyer had to do was breath. The lending institutes were not concerned about the home buyer's ability to repay the mortgage. The mortgage companies and banks were not interested in finding out the credit history, whether the appraisal was accurate, how much down payment the buyer had, what the income history of the buyer was, whether the buyer had any savings or other assets to fall back on and many other qualification requirements that should have been in place. These institutions were not concerned because they were not going to keep the loan on their books. In the majority of the cases the lender did not even receive the initial payment from the new homeowner before the mortgage was sold to another mortgage company. This would leave the new mortgage company with a mortgage that did not have the loan history. This second company would then package the loan with many others and dump them on Fannie Mae or Freddie Mac. The banks walk away since the government is now on the hook for the mortgage with no idea what the qualifications of the buyer are. This was caused by the Carter administration and given a dose of steroids by the Clinton administration. These two administrations were responsible for coming up with the idea that every American should own their own home.

The government needs to allow the Fannie Mae and Freddie Mac to go into liquidation and get out of the mortgage business entirely. They had no business guaranteeing loans in the first place. The lax policy of having the home buyer qualifying and the government that would guarantee the loan caused the largest housing crisis in the history of the United States.

The prices of homes went to outrageously high levels. These prices were not because the homes cost that much more to build but because there were thousands or even millions of people buying homes in the $150 to $250 thousand price range that did not have any possibility of making the monthly payments in the future. The real estate agents and the appraisers were working in concert with the bankers and the home buyer was left to fend for himself. The new home owner could purchase a home with little or no money down, have the closing costs included in the new mortgage and move in without any down payment in many cases. The big presentation of the real estate brokers was that you don't have to worry the value of your home will increase over the next few years? The next step to really killing the new homeowner was the Adjusted Rate Mortgage (ARM) this was the real killer for most of the new homeowners. It allowed them to over finance the purchase and have a lower payment than the rent they were used to paying. This created a false hope that this was the pot of gold at the end of the rainbow. What they did not realize was that the ARM was going to kick in within six or nine months and then the payments would start to go up until they finally reach a level that these new homeowners did not have the income to make the payments and no other assets to fall back on. Then the foreclosure notices start coming and the new homeowner is in the tank. Once the bubble started to break the value of their homes started to fall and within a month or two these people were upside down on their mortgage.

Yes, the new homeowner did not use the proper thinking process in this purchase but in many thousands of cases they were being misled by unscrupulous real estate brokers and lending institutions. The fees for processing a loan can run into several thousand dollars and the lending institutes were smiling. Yes, the homeowner needs to accept his part of the problem but the majority of the blame needs to go to the mortgage companies. They were the ones that were allowing the practice because they were making billions on the market.

The banks need to be responsible for the majority of these losses because they did not use any sound business practice or prudent lending policies when making these loans. They need to repossess all of the loans and honestly report the losses on their financial statements. The big banks are once again making excessive profits of the customers with over draft charges and other fees that only affect the lower income families. How many rich people do you know that are paying charges of $35.00 per check overdraft? What I would like to know is just how many repossessions are being carried on the banks book as a past due loan instead of honestly reporting them as mortgages that are in foreclosure proceedings? When you think about this it reminds me of the early 1930's when the banks took over the majority of the real estate for pennies on the dollar. Could we be headed into the same type scenario? The government needs to pass legislation that will force Fannie Mae and Freddie Mac to enter into a liquidation phase and then they need to get out of the mortgage business and let the business either make the proper type of loans or suffer the losses. These banks were in bed with the regulating agencies and sold massive amounts of bad loans to Fannie Mae and Freddie Mac and made unrealistic profits with the mortgage backed security transactions and they knew that the securities were worthless.

When the banks start showing massive losses and are on the verge of running out of money the government does not need to even think about bailing them out. They created their own mess and deserve to solve the problem by their own means. Sell more shares of the bank, lower the banks executive officers salaries and do the same cost cutting procedures every other successful business would do.

The United States government needs to get out of the mortgage business completely. The government does not have any business trying to control the mortgage markets or the housing markets. We are a free enterprise system that needs to be allowed to be free.

CHAPTER TWENTY THREE

Foreclosure Crisis

The foreclosure crisis is not going to help any of the homeowners that are facing foreclosure get refinancing so that they can remain in their homes. The issue is about the creditability of the lending institutes in their processing of the loan documents. The whole mess was caused by realtors, appraisers, mortgage companies and the governments mandate that every American should own a home. This was first implemented by the Carter administration and then given steroids by the Clinton administration.

The idea that every American should own a home is ludicrous. When someone wants to own a home they need to know how they are going to pay for the home. What ever happened to the requirement of a reasonable down payment? How about proof of income so that the lending institute will know that you have the means to make the payments? What about back up funds in case of emergency or termination from employment? These questions were not being asked because no one cared. Then the loan documents were transferred to another lender and the paperwork did not always follow. The lenders became lax and didn't read the majority of the documents to see if they were in order and rubber stamped their approval.

The lending institutes really were after making the profits from the initial filing fees and could have cared less about whether the loan would be repaid. They knew that they were going to sell the loan to another mortgage company and then the next mortgage company would package the loan with others and sell them to Fannie Mae or Freddie Mac. They were under the impression that they were off the hook for the mortgage.

If the homeowner had done what the mortgage and banking industry has done they would be accused of fraud and embezzlement and prosecuted to the fullest extent of the law. Why can the mortgage and banking institutes practice these fraudulent procedures then get a free ride and are not prosecuted? What happened to everyone being equal before the law? The abuse of the law by politically powerful banks undermines one of the key tenets of the American way.

Deutsche Bank National Trust filed to foreclose on a homeowner even though it had sold the mortgage to Goldman Sachs. This would mean that it did not have any legal right to foreclose. One judge found that about half of the motions filed in his court were so full of errors that he refused to approve them.

The documents that are filed in court are the foundation of our legal system. A signed affidavit is legally equivalent to providing live testimony in court. If an affidavit is untrue, that's the same as lying in court, which is a crime called perjury.

Yet the current system is filled with thousands of cases where the banking industry used documents that were fraudulently submitted to the court that were certified as accurate when they were in fact not. Attorneys are prohibited from making a material misrepresentation to the court, it's clear that such misrepresentations of fact are widespread in foreclosure proceedings.

In the good old days, when a bank issued a mortgage they would hold the loan as an asset and collect the interest and principal payments from the homeowner. But Wall Street banks divided the payments that go toward interest and loan principal into slices, which were assembled by risk and rate of return into pools of mortgages that were then sold as a single security. With the mortgages divided into pieces that were then bundled into securities that were bought and sold numerous times, the ownership of the underlying mortgage and home often became muddled. This is how two different companies can end up filing foreclosure documents on the same house.

Every time this type of securities changed hands, the various claims on the underlying house should have been transferred as well. In many cases, they weren't. In some cases, foreclosures have been allowed even when the original mortgage has been lost. If you don't need the original document to take someone's home, then exactly what rule of law is at work in America?

The flawed foreclosure documents are going to drag out the housing slump for several years. The uncertainty of not knowing how many foreclosed homes are going to be on the market is going to continue to drag the home prices even lower. The sale of foreclosed homes is going to be severely damaged due to the integrity of the documents. Why would anyone want to buy a home not knowing whether the legal documents could be adequate to provide title insurance?

With millions of foreclosed homes on the market that cannot be sold with clear titles, then that will effectively freeze a significant portion of the American real estate market. After all, about a third of all home sales involve residences in default or foreclosure.

Fannie Mae and Freddie Mac have been pulling foreclosed homes off the market, canceling signed deals and removing properties from inventory of unsold homes. Homeowners already in the foreclosure process are now wondering whether the impending foreclosure situation will delay or even cancel their impending eviction notices.

Most Americans have not trusted the lending institutes for many years with regard to their fairness and maneuvering of the legal system for their benefit. The points system and closing costs created huge profits for the lenders. All were demanded up front to provide the banks with substantial profits.

The foreclosure problems are going to last for several years and the economy is going to be held back from a quick and sustained recovery. The housing market and jobs are the key factors that are going to keep our economy improving at a snails pace.

America's home foreclosure crisis may have faded from the front page headlines, but that doesn't mean the problem has gone away. Consider the situation in Modesto, California, a city of more than 210,000 people located about 90 miles east of San Francisco. According to RealtyTrac an online service that markets foreclosed properties, Modesto had the nation's third-highest home foreclosure rate during the third quarter of 2010, just behind Las Vegas, Nevada, and Cape Coral/Fort Meyers, Florida.

In practical terms, that means one in 36 homes in Modesto is in foreclosure and the evidence of this is visible from street level. You won't find entire blocks of Modesto that stand vacant -- it's still not Detroit, after all -- but in practically every neighborhood and on every street, there's usually at least one house that's been foreclosed. It's pretty easy to spot: Amid the neatly manicured lawns and landscapes of Modesto's streets, foreclosed homes are the ones where the lawn has gone feral, the shades in the windows sit askew, and rows of legal notices are taped to the windows near the front door.

"We're going to be near the top of the foreclosure list for a long time," says Bob Johnson of Direct Appraisals in Modesto. "The majority of the foreclosures here are people who used home equity loans to buy cars and other things. Banks often try to help out with loan modifications, but that doesn't really help, so people just walk away. Bottom line is, people here say they just won't pay mortgages that are worth more than the value of the property."

Oddly, however, despite Modesto's high rate of foreclosure, some new home construction continues. At a brand-new subdivision called The Arbors at Graham Estates, workers pour concrete for new foundations, just yards away from a row of newly completed homes. Prices here start at $230,000 for a 1600 square-foot house, and according to Tim Parish, the project superintendent for developer Frontier Community Builders, the new units are selling well, even though foreclosures often sell for half as much. Foreclosed homes are often plagued by mold infestation, damaged walls, and broken appliances. Even in a market like this, some people just don't want a used car.

It will be a very long time before Modesto will escape the havoc caused by the foreclosure crisis. "We see all kinds of properties, even homes bought in 2008." says Omar Perez, an appraiser with Cal Valley Appraisers. "It's going to be like this for a few more years, and that will keep a lot of downward pressure on values. Home values will eventually climb again, but I doubt we'll get to where we were in 2005 or 2006, even 10 years from now." This article was written by Todd Lappin.

Those were just a few of the comments made by people from all across the United States. There were thousands of other replies that I decided not to use due to the nature of the postings. About 90% of them were one sentence that contained many misspelled words and usually had one or two of this (@#$%&) type words included in the reply. The vast majority of these comments had to be from people that were not very well educated and the majority leaned towards the Democratic viewpoint.

Underwater homes in the United States

CHAPTER TWENTY FOUR

My Loan Program

The problem created by the excess homes available in the real estate market could be helped by instituting my loan program. To qualify for this program the purchaser of a home will be required to meet strict standards. The banks will be required to meet strict standards which will be difficult and probably impossible to get them to agree to accept.

The banks and lending institutions have acted irresponsibly with regard to foreclosed properties. They have failed to keep these homes repaired and in shape to be repurchased by people looking for a home that can be lived in and become respectable. The majority of the homes that have been foreclosed upon are now in a serious need of attention and this could be provided by my loan program. The lenders are going to be helped and it is going to provide a method of lowering the housing inventory.

To qualify for a loan under this program the buyer must agree to live in the home for a period of five years.

The buyer will agree to maintain the property while they are living there during this five year period. The buyer can make any major improvements with the consent of the lender. The home will be for a single family residence. The buyer will not qualify if they own another home and plan to move into the new property. The buyer will be required to make the monthly payments in a timely manner or will be disqualified. A buyer must not have more than one late payment in any given 12 month period. Should the buyer default on the terms of the loan the payments will be determined to be rent income to the lender and the sale cancelled. The buyer will become a month to month renter.

The lending institutes will provide a zero interest loan for the first 36 months. The payment will be computed upon the loan converting to a 5% interest rate at the end of the 36 months period. All the payments during the first 36 months will be the down payment on this loan. The history of the 36 months payments will improve the credit score of the buyer. The loan payment will include the taxes and insurance of the buyer and will be deducted from the amount that is credited as the down payment after the 36 months period. The lenders will be required to keep this loan on their books and not sell this mortgage. The banks are able to receive very low or interest free money from the Federal Reserve and should be using these funds to help improve our real estate problems. If the banks refuse to use the federal funds for this program they will not be allowed to borrow any more funds from the Federal Reserve.

The sale price of the property will be the fair market value of the property on the date of the transaction. Due to the condition of most foreclosed properties this is going to be a lot lower than the lenders are expecting. In all cases there will be a loss to the lenders that they will have to accept. This value will be established by independent appraisers that are not hired by the lender. The price must be fair to the purchaser so that they will have a reasonable chance for the home to stay at the current price level and not continue the serious decline of the past few years. We do not want to create more under water home loans. We want to eliminate the homes on the foreclosure market and stabilize the entire market.

An example of how the loan would work

The purchase price of the home is $200,000 which is established by independent appraisers that do not have any connection to the lender. The interest rate would be zero percent for the first 36 months but the payment would be computed using an interest rate of 5%. The loan will convert to a fixed 30 year mortgage at the end of the 36 months period. There will not be a requirement for a down payment. There will be requirements that the purchaser provides proof of income and has a reasonable credit score.

The monthly loan payment would be $1,275.00.

36 Months at $1,275.00 would equal $45,900.00.

Estimated Real Estate Taxes and Insurance $6,000.00.

Balance for Down Payment upon conversion to a 30 year fixed mortgage would be $39,900.00. This figure would be subtracted from the $200,000.00 purchase price and the new mortgage would be for $160,100.00. This will provide the purchaser with what amounts to a 19.95 percent equity and establishes a track record of making payments. An additional advantage to the purchaser would be that the loan would be paid off in less than the 30 years because the payment would be more than required for a loan of $160,100.00. It will help with the glut of foreclosed homes on the market. The lender will be required to provide title insurance at the end of the 36 month period at no cost to the purchaser.

CHAPTER TWENTY FIVE

Reduce the Government Payroll

The following information was extracted from the Internet. I do not know who wrote the article but it is right on concerning some of the problems that are happening in government employment sector. This information if provided to make everyone think about our government payrolls and unemployment.

In New York, a 44-year-old firefighter retires with a $101,000 a year pension, for life. Near Chicago, a parks commissioner quits and begins collecting a $166,000 pension – a sum sweetened by $50,000 thanks to a one-time retirement year windfall of $270,000. And in California, a former city manager pulls down $500,000 in retirement checks every year.

As outrageous as those sunset stipends may seem, they are merely the most visible piece of what critics of generous government pensions say is a ticking time bomb of debt that is threatening to bankrupt a number of states by the end of the decade.

While the federal debt of $13.7 trillion raises issues of devalued currency, higher borrowing costs for Washington, D.C., and loss of international bargaining power, state debt – much of it driven by exploding pension costs – poses a more immediate risk to the United States economy, according to many experts.

Wall Street analyst Meredith Whitney correctly predicted the need for a government bailout of banks three years ago, so people listened in September when she forecast who will be next to beg for a federal bailout: States like California, New Jersey and Ohio. State and local governments have effectively run up huge credit card bills, and soon won't even be able to make the minimum payments on that debt. What happens then? Middle America, Whitney predicted in a report called "Tragedy of the Commons," might revolt at the idea at bailing out coastal states for years of mismanagement and overspending.

Crushing debts racked up by these and other states are obvious almost every budget year, when state government shutdowns are threatened and tax increases loom. But annual budget woes are a drop in the bucket compared to long-term obligations facing these states – particularly their promises to supply pensions and health care to millions of retired workers. Pension talk might not sound sexy, but it should: U.S. states already are short $1 trillion they should have set aside to pay retired workers, according to the Pew Center on the States. That hole could very well drive states to bankruptcy or federal bailout.

As documented in our continuing series on super sized government worker pay, granting super sized pensions seems irresponsible in light of this looming fiscal catastrophe. Yet, in California alone, nearly 10,000 retirees will get pension checks totaling at least $100,000 this year.

The economic struggles of the past decade lit the fuse for the pension fund time bomb. In 2000, half of the 50 states had enough money socked away to cover future pension costs, according to Pew. By 2008, only four states -- Florida, New York, Washington and Wisconsin -- could make that claim. The other 46 are potentially on the road to insolvency.

Joshua Rauh, associate professor of finance at at Northwestern University, estimates that 20 states will run out of pension money by 2025.

The pension doomsday clocks in Illinois and New Jersey will strike even sooner, in 2018. What happens then? In New Jersey, for example, the state is obligated to pay pensions out of the general fund when the pension fund runs dry. In 2018, the state will owe $14 billion in pension payouts, or one-third of the state's annual tax receipts. To put that in perspective, to plug a budget hole like that this year, the state would have to cut all education spending. That bears repeating: It would have to eliminate spending on every elementary school, high school and college from its budget.

That's why stories of $195,000 pensions, rampant double-dipping, workers collecting pensions on seven, eight or even nine government jobs, and other excesses seem so absurd.

And pension gamesmanship is routine around the country. For example, pension payments are often based on the employee's salary in the final year on the job, or final three years. That formula is easily abused, a process sometimes called "back-ending." A pension commission in New Jersey found one worker spent 24 years in public service earning less than $10,000, then one year as a prosecutor earning $141,000. That boosted his pension from $3,600 to $70,000 annually. The employee wasn't named.

There are probably as many variations as you can imagine. Just when we think that we've heard something amazing, I'll hear something more amazing. It goes on everywhere across the country. It's human nature; if you can figure out a way to inflate your pension, you are going to do it. People who make a career of it are making out like bandits.

Another common pension abuse is "double-dipping" – a practice in which employees retire and start collecting their pension, and then they are rehired to perform their old job at their old salary. It's a common practice for government workers around the country, despite many rules forbidding it. Workers often argue that they have earned their pension and their right to retire, and if they decide to work during retirement, they're entitled. But the logic there is deeply flawed.

Pensions were designed to make sure government workers were allowed to grow old with dignity, not to make them rich.

In this series on super-sized government pay, we've already met Phoenix police chief/public safety manager Jack Harris, who's become the nation's poster child for "double-dipping." He retired as chief in 2007 and began collecting a $90,000 pension. Two weeks later, he was hired for essentially the same job, re-titled "public safety manager," and granted a salary of $193,000. Harris attracted nationwide attention after a lawsuit was filed by conservative interest group Judicial Watch. The lawsuit claims the public safety manager's job was manufactured expressly to circumvent both pension rules and a state law aimed at curbing the practice.

Peter Tom is a municipal compensation specialist who's worked in New Jersey's complicated government worker environment for three decades. New Jersey even has rules designed to enable double-dippers, he said. Yet, he's seen all manner of pension-stuffing through the years.

This would not be allowed in the private sector because the pension committees are third party administrators who have fiduciary responsibilities.

While the outrage factor on six-figure pensions and lucrative loopholes is high, there is a more practical, actuarial problem: Pension recipients aren't paying their fair share, creating unfunded liabilities. For example, a worker who pays 5 percent of a $10,000 salary into the system for 24 years, then 5 percent of a $140,000 salary for one year, doesn't cover the costs of a $70,000 pension.

These loopholes create unfunded liabilities that have helped damage the pension pool. Pensioners are never asked to make up the difference.

In truth, pension systems rely on what might be considered an accounting trick, not unlike the trick which keeps the Social Security system afloat for now. While state workers contribute payments to the system – typically about 5 percent of their salary -- and those payments are matched by government employers -- about 10 percent -- those payments scarcely cover the eventual payouts. You can never pay enough to pay for your retirement.

In fact, "defined benefit" pension plans make no direct connection between the worker's contributions and the benefits enjoyed later. Pension systems hope for large investment gains during a worker's career – in many states the calculations project an annual return of around 8 percent, a fantasy -- but really rely on the payments of current workers to fund payouts to retired workers.

Just as pensions are a bit of an accounting trick (or a Ponzi scheme, some might argue), pension obligations do not appear on state balance sheets as debts. If they did – if states actually had to write down what they owe retirees going forward, and assume a modest return on investments -- the unfunded portion of the payments could be as high as $4.3 trillion. That's nearly a third of the federal debt, which currently stands at $13.7 trillion. The federal government's massive debt steals headlines, vaults politicians to office and has its own Times Square clock, but at least Washington, D.C., can print money. Meanwhile, states are staring at a huge mammoth black hole with seemingly no way to dig out.

While the contribution formulas have systematic flaws, their shortcomings are severely exacerbated by another simple math problem – life expectancy has jumped almost 10 years since 1960.

Unions managed to lower or reduce the retirement age while increasing benefits in a period of history where people are living longer. So you begin seeing what the problem is.

There is a police chief who will pull in $5 million in California before he is projected to die.

Most pension reformers are calling for state governments to switch to a defined contribution system, similar to 401(k) plans many workers have. That would mean workers would only get what they put into the system -- combined with any employer cash contributions and supplemented by investment gains -- when they retire.

But while that is fiscally responsible from the government's point of view, a defined contribution plan is a meager replacement for a defined benefit plan. That's why unions are putting up quite a fight against pension reform.

Here's a simple rule-of-thumb comparison. A 30-year government worker with a final salary of $80,000 could expect an annual pension of roughly $55,000, or about $4,600 per month for life, under the current scheme.

To earn that kind of guaranteed monthly income, a 401(k) saver would need $1 million in their retirement account, assuming $100,000 in savings can generate $400 in monthly income.

While it's not impossible to grow a 401(k) to those lofty levels, it is rare. In fact, 50 percent of Americans who have 401(k) accounts have less than $35,000 in them. Contrast that with our 30-year government workers who can all expect predictable pension checks.

So expect a furious battle as state governments attempt to reign in pension costs.

But in the end, pensions are about power. Elected officials from local and state governments maintain power by doling out favors and perks, and there is no perk like a pension.

The governments need to enact legislation that the employee that is double dipping is removed from their current job. We have unemployment reported by the government of 9.8% in the United States. The real number of people unemployed is more like 20% when you consider all those that have decided to quit looking for work and those that have used up all of their benefits.

These double dipping employees should be required to resign so that the younger generation of employees can be hired to fill the positions that are being occupied by the double dippers. This will provide for two things. First, it will reduce the government payrolls by letting newer employees enter the market at lower pay rates than the double dippers. Second, it will allow the government to reduce the number of employees due to the fact that they would only have to replace the ones that are actually required to be functional. We need for the government to reduce the size of the work force by at least 20 – 25 percent. There is at least that much waste in the governments operations.

The detection of the double dippers will be very easy to accomplish. Every employee that files an income tax return that reports retirement income and received a Form 1099 could be detected. When they file a return that has a W-2 from current government employment as well they would have their name placed into a data bank. If they do not voluntarily resign the government could release them with cause and fine them $25,000. The fine will deter these employees from double dipping. This will make every union member scream bloody murder.

The other part of the problem is the governments needing to be union controlled. If the government is such a great place to work, why are the unions needed anyway?

Comments from the citizens

The retirement systems need to be updated to eliminate the unfairness of back loading. Using your three highest salary years average is costly but maybe 5 years would be better. Returning to your same job after you have retired should not be permitted under any circumstance. If you get an entirely different job with the state at a lower salary, I don't think would be a problem. People who want to work should work and their experience and expertise should not be lost. Also, the longer you are in a system, the better your retirement benefits should be. Free health care after 5 years service is stupid! You should work for the state for at least 25 to 30 years to get covered healthcare. And pension monies should never be a part of the general budget of a state. Look what the politicians and their cronies have done in the states that are facing bankruptcy in the not too distant future.

At least the state pension plans have only 23.4%, on average, of their investments in government and corporate bonds. The federal employees have 100% invested in Treasuries, and tapping them is no different than paying for battleships. It is literally pay-as-you-go. The existence of the trust fund makes it no easier to pay benefits than if the trust fund didn't exist. The same can be said for Social Security.

There are links and excerpts from reputable governmental agencies to back up my statements to those who are interested.

Those who retire then come back and are getting retirement income as well as getting paid (double dippers) have no concern for younger generations that need good jobs to support their family. The double-dippers I have seen in our county here don't have skills that can't be done by an existing employee. Give existing workers the opportunity and encouragement to do a portion of that job. Distribute the tasks over existing positions. I guarantee there are existing employees who will do it faster and better.

You are already paying benefits to those existing employees and can offer a raise to them.

In the past, I worked a state employee in Alaska & Washington State, in the same division and capacity. The examples used in this article are extreme and only provoke the reader, without them knowing that many of us are receiving modest monthly retirement checks. While I earned a higher income in Alaska during the 1980's, our pay raises were modest. After I accepted an early retirement and relocated to Washington State, I accepted a rather substantial reduction in pay and learned raises would be next to nil for the next 15 years. In this day and age when many retirees face a reduced social security benefit because they receive a pension to which they contributed, giving extreme examples of wealth only incite the reader. It is no wonder Americans are angry and perplexed, as what is presented as 'news' and/or 'fact' is neither. Unfortunately, many see the glass as half empty, rather than half full depending on their circumstance. I am an elder and concerned for many I know who continue to be tireless public servants who work on behalf of others.' I wonder what will become of the contributions they've poured into the public retirement coffers. The answer to all of this is to do away with all these pension plans and put all of them on Social Security. After all we poor people on Social Security are the ones who bail them out and pay for their pensions. Why should the crooks get more than the honest people we need to revolt and make one pension plan the goal? We would certainly not hear all this crap about Social Security not being funded as the skimmers would be paying their fair share hopefully.

I heard that Wall Street contacted the Republicans the day after the election to let them know what they wanted in return for all of the money they had put into the election for them. They want the financial bill to prevent them from crashing our economy again repealed! So, put all of the state pensions in the hands of Wall Street and privatize Social Security by putting that in the hands of Wall Street. They get to charge you for every little thing, and then wipe you out with greedy speculation. What a great plan for the seniors? Not!

We had a man by the name of Steve Cooley running for Attorney General in this last election. If he is not elected (still counting ballots) I presume he will continue his current employment as District Attorney for Los

Angeles Co. There was a political ad in which he said if he was elected, he would collect his pension for his job as District Attorney to supplement his Attorney General income of $150,000/year. Would sure like to know what his salary is for being the District Attorney.

What about our elected congress men & women, state and federal, who get to vote themselves a raise any time they want and we don't get any say at all? Bet you won't see them voting themselves a pay cut to help with the budget.

Marin County, California is owned lock, stock and barrel by the unions (all democrats) has a population of 200,000. We have 19 school districts, 13 police departments 17 fire districts with $200 - 300k salaried "chiefs and superintendents" and their staffs. The "unfunded pension liabilities" have ballooned from $250mm in 2004 to over $2billion today. The largest employer in the County is...you guessed it the County and the public employee unions. The unions (and the Democrats they, the environmentalists and bicyclists) OWN their bosses...contribute massively to local elections like the other "first to go bankrupt in the Country Bay area counties: Sonoma, San Mateo, Contra Costa and San Juaquin. God help us...it may be simply too late.

These big pensions make me so irritated. I go to work every day in the private sector and I don't make a lot of money at all. Once money is taken out for taxes, health insurance (which continues to go up) and my 10% contribution to my 401k (which is no longer matched by my company due to the current economic condition) I really don't get a big pay check at all. I don't have excessive sick or vacation days or summers off or fall breaks or anything like that. My pay actually went down last year because of the market. I hear people complaining about pay freezes, but welcome to the real world where you don't expect pay increases and actually get reductions because that is reality. These pension plans are completely out of control and the people that make the rules are the ones that benefit from them and so I don't see any end in sight. Of course – who would not want one of these plush pensions to rely on and not have to worry everyday about saving and if the stock market is going to crash? A lot of people in the private sector are barely making enough to pay the bills, let alone put money in a 401k. The reality is – these pensions are too plush and are costing tax payers too much. "We contend that for a nation to try to tax itself into prosperity is like a man standing in a bucket and trying to lift himself up by the handle" Winston Churchill. It's only fair to get what you put in and clearly this current system just isn't fair or working at all.

This gravy train has got to stop. This absolutely absurd! These government pensions are economically unsustainable, period. When these pensions were first formulated, government workers (cops, firemen, teachers and other government workers) used to make a salary that was generally lower than wages in the private sector, often a lot lower. But that is no longer true and it hasn't been for a long time. The government unions got smart -- they "get the vote out" and use their huge union war chests to support politicians, who in turn rubber stamp their cushy government contracts with their mandatory pay raises and their Cadillac health plans and other benefits. It's the biggest back-scratching scheme of all time. We in the private sector have to work and save for our own retirement. I've been working full time since I was 22. I expect to work until I'm 65 (that is, I hope to retire at 65, but I'm not sure if I'll be able too). That's 43 years. I don't feel like working any longer than I have to because I have to pay huge amounts in taxes to cover government workers, many of whom retired after only 20 years of working, juiced up their pension benefits by working incredible amounts of overtime in the last two years before retiring and engaged in these other "legal" schemes we hear about. I don't care if the government was negligent in not putting enough away each year to fund these retirement plans. That's not the point! The point is that these pension benefits are insanely too high. This article had it exactly right when it said that pensions were first designed so that government workings could retire and grow old with dignity; they were not designed to make people rich. Government workers sit there and say "What do you mean? We're not rich." I've got news for you, compared almost all of us in the private sector, yes you are. The amount of money that we have to save when we retire so that we are sure we have guaranteed income for the rest of our lives like government workers is in the millions -- and most of us don't and won't have millions. We in the private sector have been asleep and suckers for too long. It's time to wake up!!!!!!!!! They will fight us, of course they will -- tooth and nail. You would too if you had this pension gig and someone was threatening to take it away from you. But I'm ready for all out war to fight this insanity; I don't care how long they strike, I don't care if I have to home school my kids -- this insanity has to stop!!!!! The majority of us in the private sector shouldn't have to work for over 40 years so the minority in the government sector can retire worry free after only working for 20 to 25 years.

I have always believed you should only get what you put in -- I'm talking retirement, social security, life, work, love, etc. I have not paid much into retirement, because I didn't have much to pay in, and when I retire, I don't expect to live like a king. Americans no longer have ethics. It is really sad that so many people truly that stealing is OK.

I live in New Jersey and have a combined pension and Social Security disability of $1700 a month. My Sister and her crooked husband both worked for the so called State under the pension system they have and they are both pulling in over $5400 a month in pensions? I only worked in the private sector for most of my life and my Real Estate Taxes on this modest (800 square foot) home is 8 cents short of $6000 per year? The systems are so out of whack, that I can not believe it. Politicians only look out for themselves and until I see some real change...like some fairness in the system...I will never believe that anything will change.

Firefighters, at least in California, make too much for what they do anyway. How about we compare the amount of calls to 911 for a medical problem to how many calls for a fire? Between 80-90% of all 911 calls are medical in nature. The vast majority of private sector paramedics (which make up most of all of the paramedics in California) out there make less than half of the average firefighter's salary, yet do the majority of the work - who transports, and stays with the patient, and does the majority of treatment. Firefighters have had it good for a very, very long time - they have fought to get a great paying job with great benefits and are now reluctant to give that up. In San Diego, there was an article that described how Captains would be promoted to a Battalion Chief position for a very short time, then move back down to Captain, just so that they could get an additional jump in there pension when they retire - they get paid based on the highest rate of pay they received when they were on the job, i.e. chief pay, 6 figures. Recently, government job pay exceeded private sector pay, this shouldn't be happening. Everyone has been tightening their belts around here and it's time for the firefighters to do the same.

The problem is not the pension benefit but how it is administered. The highest 3 year benefit mark should be based on regular pay not overtime, that would take care of a lot of the padding. Double dipping which is not supposed to be allowed is simple. If you retired and are drawing a government pension and want to return to the work force fine, you cannot however join any type of new government pension plan. Most government workers would stay at their current job longer if there was not a way to double dip, and most work until a normal retirement age anyway. It is the minority of government workers that are causing the problem. We have come to the point of no matter where you work there is corruption, no way around it. We need to look at ourselves and our neighbors and work together to fix our problems. A good start to fix America is to stop trying to fix the World! We pay for everybody else's problems, there are enough taxes paid in to clean things up if we kept the money at home.

I retired from the state after 30 years of service. What I have seen in state government is that the ones who have political connections are the ones offered newly created (consultant) positions within the same department after retirement. If there were laws that prevented anyone that has retired from a city, state or federal job preventing them form working in any government position again would stop some of this political back scratching abuse.

This country is in a period where all the financial laws need to be rewritten. Congress needs to come to the governments rescue with fair adjustments on pensions. The government had to do this to UAW and needs to relieve the governments of a system that threats the nation. It is time for Congress to stop bickering and simplify issues and solve one issue at a time.

In Florida, despite the propaganda, the pension is so well-funded that it only uses 1% of the state budget a year. There are many of us who don't make lots of money, and won't get a big pension. We will have to depend on it, pay our own health insurance, and hope Social Security is not cut. I stuck with my employer for over 35 years because I was hoping to have a secure old age. I have worked in the private industry by the way. My job is no easier now. In Florida you must be retired a year before you can even volunteer for a job that has state retirement without losing your benefits. This is a new law. It used to be one month. A lot of politicians may double dip, but not us ordinary folks.

They should all be fired...Living off the tax dollars of hard working

Americans who can barely afford the essentials...we don't need higher taxes, we need to cut the greed. From the federal level on down...they make me sick! This will continue until the American people rise up and say no more.

Double dipping in the cases I am familiar with meant that people retired knowing they could double dip. They were then paid their retirement pay plus their pay from being hired back. In one case, they came back as consultants plus got their retirement. It is not sustainable to pay a person $75K in retirement pay to not do the job and then pay them another $75K to do the same job.

The employees of the federal government have been a huge expense to the American taxpayers for way to long. The salaries of all federal employees should be reduced by a minimum of twenty five (25%). This would affect every government employee that is earning in excess of $40,000 per year. The one exception would be the people involved in the security of the United States. This will bring the cost of running the government down and decrease the deficit that has been predicted in the proposed budget. We know this is going to be a real difficult piece of legislation to get through the Congress.

To provide some information why the federal employees should receive a huge pay cut. The federal employees have been enjoying a boom in their compensation and employment. While the private sector of our economy was loosing 7 million jobs the federal employees increased by around 100,000 employees. The number of federal employees that are earning over $110,000 per year has increased from 14 percent to 19 percent of their workforce.

The average compensation of a federal employee in now $123,000 per year and that does not count their benefits. That is more than double what the same type employees are earning in the private sector of our economy. Reports indicate that four out of the five jobs that President Obama claimed were created by the stimulus bill were for government employees.

Doesn't everyone think that it is about time for the federal employees to share in the difficulties the rest of the citizens are experiencing?

In addition the house Democratic leadership has refused to consider a bill that would reduce the salaries of the Congressional representatives by a measly 5%. All of us should also be aware that it has been 77 years since the Congress voluntarily took a pay cut. They are not only over paid they should be required to take a substantial pay cut.

Any employee that does not want to accept the reduction in their salary should enter into retirement or be discharged from the service of the government. The government has grown to uncontrollable proportions and needs to be reduced. The senior managers in the government need to start better management and production controls and make sure that every government employee is actually earning his income. There is an exceptional amount of dead weight in the government and this will help weed out the non productive employees.

The members of Congress will receive the following salaries for 2010. All members will receive $174,000 with the minority and majority leaders receiving $193,400. The Speaker of the House will receive $223,500. By reducing these figures by 25% the government will save $4,122,025.

Division of Government	Annual Salary	25% Savings
The Presidents Czars	$7,400,000	1,850,000
The Congress	9,088,100	2,272,025
Total		$4,122,025

The portion of the federal budget that goes to pay the government payroll is buried in each section of the proposed budget to make it very difficult to extract. We are going to suggest that the government decrease the discretionary spending parts of the 2011 proposed budget by 10%. This is such a small percentage that every division should be able to manage without creating any hardships. Just good old fashioned management skills will make this occur. These figures come from the content of the 2011 proposed budget presented by the President. We can balance the budget by forcing every department to tighten up the belt and become conservative instead of spending money they do not have. This is an attempt to come as close as we can to show the American people just how much money is wasted or spent without anyone knowing what it was spent for.

In order to do this we will break down the cost per division of the budget. These figures are in millions.

Discretionary Spending	Amount	10% Savings
Department of Agriculture	$27,143	2,714
Department of Commerce	8,928	893
Department of Defense	708,255	70,825
Department of Education	49,697	4,970
Department of Energy	31,609	3,161
Department of Health and Human Services	81,257	8,126
Department of Homeland Security	43,589	4,359
Department of Housing and Urban Development	41,590	4,159
Department of the Interior	12,439	1,244
Department of Justice	24,143	2,414
Department of Labor	13,967	1,397
Department of State and Other International Programs	54,662	5,466
Department of Transportation	77,588	7,759

Department of the Treasury	13,738	1,374
Department of Veterans Affairs	55,967	5,596
Corps of Engineers —Civil Works	4,881	488
Environmental Protection Agency	10,020	1,002
National Aeronautics and Space Administration	19,000	1,900
National Science Foundation	7,424	742
Small Business Administration	1,233	123
Social Security Administration	12,142	1,214
Corporation for National and Community Service	1,416	142
Actual Total	$1,300,688,000,000	130,068

If the government would cut their spending across the board by a 10% Austerity Program and it would save the federal Government a total of $130,068,000,000 during the fiscal year ending September 30, 2011. I find it hard to believe that any branch of the government can not cut 10% out of their budget.

Other items in the budget that could use some trimming included in the Agriculture Department there are allowances for Provides $7.6 billion for the Special Supplemental Nutrition Program for Women, Infants, and Children (WIC) to serve all eligible individuals. It also provides $10 billion over 10 years or a $1 billion per year for a strong Child Nutrition and WIC reauthorization.

The following item is almost enough to make a normal person start

laughing. Where are those 20,000 border patrol troops that Obama has included in his 2011 proposed budget? The last I heard they were going to send 1,200 troops to the Southern Border. The real problem with that deployment is that they are not allowed to arrest anyone or deport anyone. That just about makes them useless. The President needs to get some courage and recommend legislation that will allow for the deportation of all the 20 million illegals that are free loading on the government of the United States and the American people.

The unfortunate part is that the President does not want to deport any illegal. There must be some subversive plan to start granting amnesty to these illegals in the hopes that they will remember what a wonderful gift the President gave them and vote for the Democrats. The citizens of America can not let any type of amnesty happen. We do not want to become a third world country. The following is from the Presidents budget.

Strengthens Border Security and Immigration Verification Programs.

The Budget includes funding to support 20,000 Border Patrol agents and complete the first segment of Customs and Border Protection's (CBP's) virtual border fence. The Budget also includes funding for 300 new CBP officers for passenger and cargo screening at ports of entry, as well as expansion of pre-screening operations at foreign airports and land ports of entry. The Budget provides more than $1.6 billion for Immigration and Customs Enforcement programs to expeditiously identify and remove from the United States illegal aliens who commit crimes. Included in this total is continued support for the Secure Communities program. To enhance and expand immigration related verification programs, the Budget provides $137 million to the U.S. Citizenship and Immigration Services. Through E-Verify, U.S. employers can maintain a legal workforce by verifying the employment eligibility of their workers, while Systematic Alien Verification for Entitlements (SAVE) assists Federal, State, and local benefit-granting agencies with determining eligibility for benefits by verifying immigration status. These programs promote compliance with immigration laws and prevent individuals from obtaining benefits for which they are not eligible.

DANGER – PUBLIC WARNING

TRAVEL NOT RECOMMENDED

- **Active Drug and Human Smuggling Area**

- **Visitors May Encounter Armed and Smuggling Vehicles Traveling at High Rates of Speed**

- **Stay Away From Trash, Clothing, Backpacks, and Abandoned Vechicles**

- **If You See Suspicious Activity, <u>Do Not Confront</u> Move_ Away and Call 911**

- **BLM Encourages Visitors To Use Public Lands North to Interstate 8.**

This a billboard just across the Mexican border in Arizona. It is how the government secures our border

Increases Funding for the Housing Choice Voucher Program.

The President's Budget requests $19.6 billion for the Housing Choice Voucher program to help more than two million extremely low to low-income families with rental assistance to live in decent housing in neighborhoods of their choice. The Budget continues funding for all existing mainstream vouchers and provides flexibility to support new vouchers leased in 2009 and 2010 and $85 million in special purpose vouchers for homeless families with children, families at risk of homelessness, and persons with disabilities. The Administration remains committed to working with the Congress to focus the goals and objectives of the program, as well as address the program's costly inefficiencies, and to fully utilize available funding by alleviating the administrative burdens on the Public Housing Authorities that implement HUD voucher and other programs, and establish a funding mechanism that is transparent and predictable in order to serve more needy families.

When will the president learn that the way to get people in a position to pay their own way is to stop giving them rent and benefits for nothing? Create the jobs that were promised in the campaign speeches and get the unemployment rates back to the acceptable range. When the government provides the necessities for people it takes away the incentive to take care of them self.

The illegals leave mile after mile of trash along their route into the United States. These types of beautification projects are completed by thousands of illegals crossing into the United States and goes on for miles and miles. Do you think it is something that the American citizens of this country really want?

CHAPTER TWENTY SIX

The Wars

The United States has been engaged in two wars for years. The war in Iraq has been going on for over 7 years and the war in Afghanistan has been going on for over 9 years. The wars have been a serious financial strain on the United States. We are the champions of freedom throughout the world but need to understand that the costs are tremendous.

President Obama declared in his campaign that he would end the war in Iraq on August 31, 2009. President Obama declared on that date that the war was officially over and ordered the troops home with the exception of 50,000. I find it very hard to believe that he thought that he could just wave his magic wand and the war would end. This is absolutely insane. The war will end when there has been a victory or the United States admits that they were defeated. Leaving 50,000 troops in Iraq does not seem to be an end to the war. Those troops are supposed to be there for police action and training of the Iraqi armed forces. Why is it then that they are being involved in combat operations on a continuing basis? It appears that this timed withdrawal of troops was nothing more than a political ploy to enhance the chances of gaining votes in the November elections.

We have a commander in chief that has not served one day in the military. He has changed field commanders in Iraq and Afghanistan on two different occasions because they did not think the president's policies made any military sense. He should be listening to the generals in the field since they have the experience that the president lacks.

Since President Obama declared an end to combat operations in Iraq, United States troops have waged gun battles with a suicide squads in Baghdad, dropped bombs on armed militants in Baquba and assisted Iraqi soldiers in a raid in Falluja. This does not sound like the end of a war.

The rules of engagement have not changed. Iraq does remain from time to time a dangerous place, so when our soldiers are attacked they will return fire per military orders.

When they answered a call for help from Iraqi soldiers overwhelmed in a gunfight with militants hiding in a palm grove near Baquba in Diyala province, United States troops brought in attack helicopters and F-16 jet fighters.

The F-16s dropped two bombs to help end the skirmish. They were the first bombs used in Iraq by the United States since July 2009.

Black is White. Freedom is Slavery. (Orwell, 1984) Does any of this surprise anyone? President Obama is a Marxist politician and a consummate liar, who still somehow holds onto a 41% favorable rating according to all of the polls. He hates the United States, he has said as much in his books, which bear a strange resemblance apparently to Mein Kampf in that he let his readers know in advance what he intended to do. Oh, and he hates Caucasian Americans too. That's in all of his books. Just so everyone gets the enormity of his war lies, the Virginia News Network, which broadcasts to radio stations around Virginia and is totally non-political, announced on September 23, 2010 that a full regiment of Virginia National Guard troops would soon deploy to Fort Hood Texas for combat training and then to Iraq for 444 days. Yes, the news reader said combat training, which will last until year's end, then 444 days in Iraq. Most people would say the number of days in a year is 365. Obama swears he will withdraw all of our fighting men and women by the end of 2011. I'm sure you true Obama followers can twist the numbers so they fit your Messiah's rhetoric. For the rest of us, this would appear to show the great leader means to stay in Iraq a little longer than he lets on. This does not sound like there is going to be a withdrawal of the troops by the end of 2011 as the president has stated. This is just another ploy prior to the elections to try and sway the voters.

There is a major difference in ending "combat operations" and ending combat or the war. The government plays on the ignorance of the people to win approval. I challenge any of you that believe that troops aren't armed to the teeth and face death at the hands of the "enemy" daily to take a trip to Iraq and visit our troops. The president can send Biden again and we can hope that a stray cartridge from one of those militants finds him.

President Obama seems to think that he can say what he wants but as long as one American soldier is in Iraq or Afghanistan a state of combat exist. As long as they are in harms way and the fighting continues the war has not ended. So his promise to end the combat is just smoke in the wind. President Obama will say and do anything to stay in power. But we all know he really isn't smart enough to run the country not alone the wars in Iraq and Afghanistan. Bring our troops home or commit to winning the wars. There can not be any alternative to winning.

There are still 50,000 troops in Iraq and still engaging the enemy. We are wondering how the President and the Democrats can call that a pull out and end of combat. Just goes to show that the Democrats will say or do anything to get a vote. That is except winning the war.

Although it is not in Iraq or Afghanistan this is really happening. We have tens of thousands of Muslims here in the United States in mosques that will keep trying to get Sharia law implemented in the United States. A government study shows that 20% of the mosques in the United States are peaceful and no threat while 80% of the mosques in the United States have some type of terrorist agenda. This war will never be over; they plan to take over this country from within just like they are now doing in Europe. Just watch the news media they are scared silly to say one word that offends the Muslim community and all the liberals always take the Muslims side instead of standing up for America. That says it all, if the liberals are for anything it more than likely is not good for America.

Although this does not have anything to do with the two wars it is very pertinent to all branches of the military. Some of the members of the military support the removal of the "Don't Ask, Don't Tell". It is their constitutional right to serve and fight for their country. Will it make some people uneasy? Yes, but there are thousands serving now, and there have been since 1776. The longer we as a society look for things to form division with, the longer we will be a bigoted nation. We can only eliminate prejudices by removing all thought of it. Get rid of "gay right", "Asian-American right", "African-American right", let's just stick to human rights and be done with it. Pretty soon instead of homosexuals going to Harvard, USC, and Ole Miss they will be attending "Historically Gay" Universities. Let's stop the division. You're gay? Ok, would you like to be treated normal, or would you like to have special interest groups and better tax break? Even though I am not gay, I want nothing more for everyone than civil treatment, and the ability to get a job. Everything else I can do on my own. I don't want a government hand in my life, and I don't want it in yours.

This year's United States death toll in Afghanistan the highest on record

- More than 320 American troops have died

- Roadside bombs claimed many of the victims

- Previous high was 313 in 2009

- War began shortly after 9/11 attack

Kabul, Afghanistan (CNN) -- In only eight months, 2010 has become the deadliest year for United States troops in Afghanistan, according to a CNN count of Pentagon and NATO figures.

At least 321 troops have died so far in 2010, the highest yearly toll since the conflict began nearly nine years ago. The previous high was last year's 313 American deaths.

The deaths occurred during an increase of U.S. troops in Afghanistan and fierce fighting across the nation, particularly in the southern and eastern regions. Roadside bombs were responsible for many of the combat deaths.

The conflict started after al Qaeda terrorists harbored by the Taliban government in Afghanistan attacked the United States on September 11, 2001. A United States led invasion that started a month later toppled the government.

What is disturbing is that President Barack Obama said that the United States would stay in Afghanistan until the job is done, despite his July 2011 deadline for some American troops to start coming home. The July 2011 date is a date in which, having ramped up our armed presence in Afghanistan ... we will then start gradually reducing the number of US troops and coalition troops that are inside of Afghanistan. Still the British are commenting that they should have the funds to continue to support the war for five years. Just how are we going to be pulling out the American forces by July 2011? Why the contradiction in terms of the war?

CHAPTER TWENTY SEVEN

Democrats Jumping Ship

The list of appointees of President Obama that are jumping ship is growing. It does not surprise me since they do not want to be blamed for the mess that the Democrats have or are creating. In addition, there were about 30 Senators that were willing to jump off the Democratic bandwagon to vote for the extension of the Bush tax cuts. You can bet your life that if the tax cuts were called the Obama tax cuts they would have already been passed to everyone. It is quite simple to see that the president will do or say anything if he thinks it will get him a few extra votes or to keep the status quo in the Congress. It doesn't seem to matter that he has a majority in both houses for the 25 months he has been in office. The Representatives are beginning to understand that they had better start listening to their constituents or they will not be re-elected in November or 2012.

David Axelrod was the latest to state he was leaving the White House. He stated he was going back to his beloved Chicago to work for Obama's re-election campaign. President Obama has displayed his massive ego with the statement he would be running for re-election in 2012. This is a president with an approval rating around 42% and he assumes that he will be the Democratic standard bearer with his record. A few days ago Senior Economic Advisor Lawrence Summers said he will step down at the end of the year. Others that have jumped ship are Peter Orszag who was Obama's Director of the Office of Management and Budget. Christina Romer, the head of the Council of Economic Advisors stepped down earlier this summer. There is speculation that White House Chief of Staff could be leaving soon to run for the office of Mayor of Chicago.

The fact that the mainstream media could be running interference for the president and the Democrat Party again in the wake of waning public opinion with the approaching mid-term elections coming. This could be a historic reversal of the control that the Democrats have enjoyed on both Houses of Congress.

These resignations can't be welcome. Why would the Obama White House want a wave of resignations announcements so close to a critical congressional election?

From the president's point of view, this has to be the worst possible news. It not only looks bad, but adds to the confusion that seems to have cast a pall over the whole executive branch and the sheep are leaving the flock.

It is apparent that Summers, Axelrod, and Emanuel have seen the light and want no part of a sinking ship and realize they need to jump off into a safe place.

Although all of these resignations have been explained as part of their attempt to get on with their lives they will still be considered as a negative towards the president. The good news for the ones resigning is that they will distance themselves from the administration and get into a position to take advantage of more enjoyable and significant positions in the private or public sectors. Besides they will still be able to leverage their contacts with the Obama administration.

This is an extremely important point. It is very valuable to be a former presidential aide for a president still serving in the White House. With his immense national network, just think of all the money Emanuel will be able to raise for his bid to run for the mayor of Chicago. The good old boys network will be in operation in full force to run the Daley machine.

All of the latest resignations are going to add to the reputation of the Obama administration that many other high ranking officials are going to be heading for the exits as well. This will enable others to head for the exit before the voters deliver a memorandum about President Obama's "Hope and Change". They are not going to buy into the new Obama message of "Protect the Change" agenda.

The two advisors that the President will miss the most have now declared that they are leaving. Emanuel will always be known for his Chicago style of politics and will likely leave as early as October.

The good news that President Obama can glean from these departures is that he will have someone to blame besides President Bush. Another point that should make Obama smile is that these people have been the leaders that have failed miserably in presenting programs to solve or relieve the problems with the economy, unemployment, border security and illegal immigration. The bad news will be for Harvard University if Larry Summers returns to the teach economics or business development. The University will be getting a proven loser in those departments.

We are finally getting rid of the majority of the advisors to the Obama administration. Christina Romer was the one that led the ill fated prediction that the stimulus program would hold the unemployment rate below 8 percent. While Peter Orszag, the White House budget director who recently broke with the administration and called for extension of all Bush-era tax cuts.

The assistant Treasury Secretary for financial stability who helped oversee the TARP program, Herbert Allison, announced Wednesday that he is returning to Connecticut for family reasons. If he handles his personal finances as well as the TARP his family is in desperate trouble.

In spite of all the high level resignations President Obama has been working overtime spinning these departures as normal and have nothing to do with the fact that his approval rating has dropped to the 42% range and the increase in the poverty level and unemployment levels in the United States under his watch.

What is really scary is that the White House communications director insisted everything is business as usual at the White House. We all need to hope that the President will go back on vacation before any more damage can be done. The business that has been done in the last 25 months will be remembered as programs that the American people did not want and was passed in spite of the peoples objections. We do not need any more business as usual.

The fact that so many high level appointments are leaving the ship before the mid-term elections will be viewed as major unrest in the White House due to the policy blunders.

Many people believe that these resignations are related to the administrations failures and declining fortunes. The President is lining up scapegoats that will feel the blame for the failures. Hopefully, these departures are being made by intelligent individuals that are realizing that they are in the middle of a one term President and want out while they can still take advantage of having been high positions of a sitting administration. It doesn't matter that it was for a president that will be considered one of the worst in history.

If these departing high ranking officials want to have any chance of a career as a lobbyist you must leave while the president is still in power. There is very little or no demand for lobbyist that have participated in a losing presidential election campaign. President Obama has set the stage for elimination in 2012 due to his policies of enacting bills and continued spending with no regard to what the people of the United States desires. There is no room for a dictator type president in the United States.

Richard Grenell, who served as a spokesman for four U.S. ambassadors to the United Nations, quipped that "Clearly they all wanted to spend more time with their families, right?"

It would realistic to believe that President Obama has gone back to his old style of Chicago back room politics and forced these high level appointments to resign. This way they could salvage some of their reputations instead of having them ruined by guiding policies that couldn't deliver the results that they promised. Once a person learns how to manipulate and control their appointments using the old style Chicago politics they will never revert to doing things in the appropriate manner.

I don't know how many of you remember the Carter days. The current unemployment rate is the highest since that time in history. Carter believed that if you kept raising the interest rates everything will be wonderful since the people would be receiving more income on their money. What was forgotten was that no one was able to purchase anything because they could not afford to pay the interest on a purchase that required financing. For those that are too young to have experienced the Carter years you could receive over 22% interest on a Money Market Account at any brokerage firm.

The economy has not turned around in spite of the enormous amount of money that was pumped into it by the stimulus program that was supposed to save the country.

It seems like the administration and members of Congress are brain dead. Why these people who are supposed to be looking out for the people of the United States are not able to learn from their mistakes. All they can think of is spending and more spending. They do not seem to realize that these projects have to be paid for by revenue to the government. They think that the money will just fall out of the sky. They don't understand that government doesn't create the kind of jobs that are required to get us out of the mess that they have created. Have you heard of a poor person hiring a lot of employees?

The Obama administration has lost the ability to function in a committed manner that will be coherent and able to fix the economy and other problems. It was time to cut the cord. Apparently the departing high level officials were not to keen on the new "Protect the Change" policies.

If President Obama has any hope of being re-elected in 2012 he must be very careful in his appointments to fill these positions. His legacy will turn on the big economic decisions he and his new team will make in the months ahead.

CHAPTER TWENTY EIGHT

Hope and Change

When President Obama was campaigning and using his theme of "Hope and Change" I doubt that anyone realized exactly what he meant and what was coming for the American people. I am going to give some examples of the hopes that we had for the changes we expected. Please no more changes for failed hope. The reasons that I believe Mr. Obama is going to be the worst President that has ever held the office in the United States are:

Obama promised to close Gitmo, it is still in operation

He has treated terrorists as petty criminals. He hasn't tried them in military tribunals for their war crimes. Obama is inexperienced.

Obama policies have tripled American debt taxing children who aren't yet born (remember no taxation without representation? – maybe politicians should not be able to place debt on future generations). Obama is incompetent.

The President from Illinois has supported programs that have lost 2 million jobs, permanently, according to Joe Biden, the Delaware Democratic Vice President. "It's the economy stupid." President Obama is a clueless concerning unemployment.

Obama promised an open and transparent debate on his policies. A great example is the Obamacare program, but delivered gangster-style, heavy-handed Chicago politics instead. There was not any transparency.

The President has bungled the economy.

Obama talked down America in foreign speeches. Obama is incompetent and reacts to foreign policies before the American peoples desires.

He promised an open and transparent administration. Instead we have back door Chicago politics.

Obama has failed to create jobs. Obama is incapable of supporting business programs to develop more jobs.

The President from Illinois gave a $1 trillion bailout to big business and banks, those who contributed the most to his election.

He has failed to hold unemployment to 8%, as promised: "It's the economy stupid." Obama is incompetent.

The President has bowed to every dictator he met. Obama is inexperienced.

Obama botched the management of the worst environmental disaster in history. Watch, he will take credit for capping the well.

He met in closed session with BP to get $20 billion. Maybe he could have gotten $100 billion if the meeting was in the open. Who was paid off?

Obama treats the American people with contempt. Obama does not listen to the will of the people he should have sworn to protect.

Obama golfed and vacationed his administration away during the oil spill and Christmas bombing attempt in Detroit. Obama is incompetent.

KKK leader Senator Byrd gets a state funeral that Obama attended. Obama honored and eulogized Byrd. Too bad Stalin, Mao Zedong, and Hitler didn't die on his watch Obama would have loved those three.

Obama is an embarrassment to America.

The Fundamental Transformation of America

When Obama wrote a book and said he was mentored as a youth by Frank, (Frank Marshall Davis) an avowed Communist, people said it didn't matter.

When it was discovered that his grandparents, were strong socialists who sent Obama's mother to a socialist school where she was introduced to Frank Marshall Davis. He was later introduced to young Barrack Hussein Obama, people said it didn't matter.

When people found out that Barrack Hussein Obama was enrolled as a Muslim child in school and his father and stepfather were both Muslims, people said it didn't matter.

When he wrote in another book he authored "I will stand with them (Muslims) should the political winds shift in an ugly direction", people said it didn't matter.

When he admittedly, in his book, said he chose Marxist friends and professors in college, people said it didn't matter.

When he traveled to Pakistan, after college on an unknown national passport, people said it didn't matter.

When he sought the endorsement of the Marxist Party in 1996 as he ran for the Illinois Senate, people said it doesn't matter.

When he sat in a Chicago Church for twenty years and listened to a preacher spew hatred for America and preach black liberation theology, people said it didn't matter.

When an independent Washington organization, that tracks Senate voting records, gave him the distinctive title as the "most liberal senator," people said it didn't matter.

When the Palestinians in Gaza set up a fund raising telethon to raise money for his election campaign, people said it didn't matter.

When his voting record supported gun control, people said it didn't matter.

When he refused to disclose who donated money to his election campaign, as other candidates had done, people said it didn't matter.

When he received endorsements from people like Louis Farrakhan and Mummar Kadaffi and Hugo Chavez, people said it didn't matter.

When it was pointed out that he was a total newcomer and had absolutely no experience at anything except community organizing, people said it didn't matter.

When he chose friends and acquaintances such as Bill Ayers and Bernadine Dohrn who were revolutionary radicals, people said it didn't matter.

When his voting record in the Illinois senate and in the U.S. Senate came into question, people said it didn't matter.

When he refused to wear a flag, lapel pin, and did so only after a public outcry, people said it didn't matter.

When people started treating him as a Messiah and children in schools were taught to sing his praises, people said it didn't matter.

When he stood with his hands over his groin area for the playing of the National Anthem and Pledge of Allegiance, people said it didn't matter.

When he surrounded himself in the White House with advisors who were pro-gun control, pro-abortion, pro-homosexual marriage and wanting to curtail freedom of speech to silence the opposition, people said it didn't matter.

When he said he favors sex education in Kindergarten, including homosexual indoctrination, people said it didn't matter.

Well, for all of the people that said it didn't matter I hope you are satisfied with what you have received with your choice of President of the United States of America.

CHAPTER TWENTY NINE

Protect the Change

President Obama is now creating a new rallying call. "Protect the Change"

Why would anyone in their right mind want to protect the change that has happened in the last two years? It was really annoying to us that the president made the rallying call to the "Black Caucus in Congress" what a racist remark. Why didn't Obama give a rallying call to all the Democrats instead of catering to the Black and Hispanic voters? There is nothing more disgusting than Obama trying to create division the voters of the United States and doing everything that he can to create a class structure in the United States.

We never thought we would be able to experience what the ordinary, moral German felt in the mid-1930s. In those times, the messiah was a former smooth-talking rabble-rouser from the streets, about whom the average German knew next to nothing. What they did know was that he was associated with groups that shouted, shoved, and pushed around people with whom they disagreed; he edged his way onto the political stage through great oratory and promises. Economic times were tough, people were losing jobs, and he was a great speaker. And he smiled and waved a lot. And people, even newspapers, were afraid to speak out for fear that his "brown shirts" would bully them into submission. And then, he was duly elected to office, a full-throttled economic crisis at hand [the

Great Depression]. Slowly but surely he seized the controls of government power, department-by-department, person-by-person, bureaucracy-by-bureaucracy. The kids joined a Youth Movement in his name, where they were taught what to think. How did he get the people on his side? He did it promising jobs to the jobless, money to the indigent, and goodies for the military-industrial complex. He did it by indoctrinating the children, advocating gun control, health care for all, better wages, better jobs, and promising to re-instill pride once again in the country, across Europe, and across the world.

He did it with a compliant media; did you know that? And he did this all in the name of justice and 'CHANGE'. And the people surely got what they voted for. Read your history books. Many people objected in 1933 and were shouted down, called names, laughed at, and made fun of. When Winston Churchill pointed out the obvious in the late 1930s while seated in the House of Lords in England, he was booed into his seat and called a crazy troublemaker. He was right, though. Don't forget that Germany was the most educated, cultured country in Europe. It was full of music, art, museums, hospitals, laboratories, and universities. In less than six years, a shorter time span than just two terms of a U. S. presidency, it was rounding up its own citizens, killing others, abrogating its laws, turning children against parents, and neighbors against neighbors, all with the best of intentions of course. The road to Hell is always paved with them.

As practical thinkers, that are not overly prone to emotional decisions, we have a choice: we can either believe what the objective pieces of evidence tell us (even if they make us cringe with disgust); we can believe what history is shouting to us from across the chasm of seven decades; or we can hope we are wrong by closing our eyes, having another drink, and ignoring what is transpiring around the American citizens.

We certainly do not hope that the change that Obama was referring to is comparable to the above. Although just about everything he advocates indicates he is promoting a class structure in the United States. The American people need to wake up and smell what is going on. As we have read and listened to the rhetoric that Obama has spewed across the nation we need to stop the change and not protect the changes as Obama is asking.

The majority of the Democrats that are running for office all know how to use the smear campaigns against the Republican foes. That is apparently because they do not have any proposed legislation that will be for the benefit of all Americans. The healthcare program and the stimulus are two examples of passing legislation that the majority of the citizens did not want. We do not need more of the Obama policy of change. It will increase the deficit to incredibly high numbers and Obama has already increased the deficit in 25 months by a larger amount than any other president in their entire terms.

When we look at the entire picture we need to understand that every member of the House of Representatives and Congress should be working to pass legislation that will benefit every American citizen. This does not mean to cater to the illegals by the bogus amnesty presented by Reid in the Dream Act. Do not let it pass or there will be attachments to every bill trying to further the influx of illegals and make them citizens. Get back to the program of becoming a citizen by legal means.

CHAPTER THIRTY

United States Savings Bonds

The time has come for the government to start issuing United States Savings Bonds again.

"It might be time for "Uncle Sam Needs You" We could start selling United States Savings Bonds again. We could pay a higher rate of interest than the banks are paying and the investors would have a much safer investment. One that could be easy to purchase and small enough denominations so that every American that wants to participate can. These funds could be used to repay our national debt to foreign countries."

Those of us that are old enough to remember that we all used to buy United States Savings Bonds. It would be great to bring back the tradition of the citizens of the United States purchasing the bonds? This way as the national debt to China is paid down the citizens would hold the debt. There would be very little demand from the citizens to cash in the bonds at any given time which would make it easier to handle than billions of dollars coming due at one time to a foreign country. Food for thought.

CHAPTER THIRTY ONE

Some Public Opinions

We need to approach the upcoming elections in November 2012 and need to provide as much information as possible so that all voters can make an informed choice when they vote for the politicians of their choice. These comments are from voting Americans. You can see from the content that the voting citizens are really mad at the current situation in the United States. The consensus is that America needs some drastic changes in November 2012.

Enjoy reading what people just like you and me are saying about Congress needing to tread carefully in the run-up election. These comments are coming from individuals that are not running for any office and are not politicians. It is amazing how much common sense the average American has and yet the people that are voted into office do not seem to have any. This newsletter will be a continuation of the comments made to the article "Congress to tread carefully in run-up election" in the previous newsletter.

The Washington Post babbled again today about Obama inheriting a huge deficit from Bush. Amazingly, a lot of people swallow this nonsense. So once more, a short civics lesson:

The budgets do not come from the White House. They come from

Congress and the party that has controlled the Congress since January 2007 is the Democratic Party. They controlled the budget process for FY 2008 and FY 2009, as well as FY 2010 and FY 2011. In that first year, they had to contend with George Bush, which caused them to compromise on spending when Bush somewhat belatedly got tough on spending increases. For FY 2009 though, Nancy Pelosi and Harry Reid bypassed George Bush entirely, passing continuing resolutions to keep government running until Barack Obama could take office. At that time, they passed a massive omnibus spending bill to complete the FY 2009 budgets. And where was Barack Obama during this time? He was a member of that very Congress that passed all of these massive spending bills, and he signed the omnibus bill as President to complete FY 2009. Let's remember what the deficits looked like during that period:

If the Democrats inherited any deficit, it was the FY 2007 deficit, the last of the Republican budgets. That deficit was the lowest in five years and the fourth straight decline in deficit spending. After that, Democrats in Congress took control of spending, and that includes Barack Obama, who voted for the budgets. If Obama inherited anything, he inherited it from himself. In a nutshell, what Obama is saying is...I inherited a deficit that I voted for and then I voted to expand that deficit four-fold since January 20, 2009. I know, blame Bush.

We believe that it is time Obama does the required budget proposal. It's late and past due so they can work on that as well as working on getting us back to work. They just want to secure their future while ours goes in the tank. Obama doesn't want to do a budget like all the other presidents had to. He is afraid that the numbers will ruin him and his lemmings. They want to keep us in the dark as much as possible. Actually the budget proposal is required by law.

President Obama and most Democrats want the extensions to apply only to individuals with annual incomes of less than $200,000, or joint filers earning less than $250,000. Continuing those tax cuts would add $3.1 trillion to the national debt over the next decade. The debt would rise by an additional $700 billion if tax cuts for the richest people are also extended.

As long as this level of economic illiteracy continues to exist in our nation, we are doomed to suffer the current economic malaise and high unemployment.

"It is a paradoxical truth that tax rates are too high and tax revenues are too low and the soundest way to raise the revenues in the long run is to cut the rates now. Cutting taxes now is not to incur a budget deficit, but to achieve the more prosperous, expanding economy which can bring a budget surplus." – John F. Kennedy, Nov. 20, 1962

President Obama stated. "Continuing those tax cuts would add $3.1 trillion to the national debt over the next decade." Where are his advisors coming from? That statement is absolute nonsense. Reduced taxes do not add to the national debt. Spending does. Stop spending and the national debt will go down. Furthermore, it is a fact that more people working at a lower tax rate generates more tax revenue than fewer people working at a higher tax rate. In his first month in office, President Obama placed the highest tax on tobacco in the history of this country because he said it would deter smoking. Why is it then that the President still smokes? So one can assume using Obama's logic that higher tax on wages will provide more employment. What has he been smoking?

For 4 years the American people have put up with the idiot Democrats. It's too late to hurt America anymore. Pelosi and Reid are the worst people that have ever been in charge of the House of Representatives and the Senate. Then along comes the lying Obama to top it off. November is almost here. The last 2 years have been nothing but behind closed door politics, a stupid health care bill, a wasted stimulus, the bail out of unions and banks except the 2 that donated to Obama's campaign, Freddie and Fannie, the auto workers and teachers unions made out big time with our tax payer dollars. They also screwed up on the oil spill. They have yet to secure the borders. We have had terrorist attacks in America, 2 that could have been bad if it wasn't for stupid terrorist. He doesn't seem to care about jobs till the election gets close, now all of a sudden they seem important to him. All he does is blame others for his own stupidity and his cabinet isn't much better. He talks a good talk, but nothing happens. There is only one news station that will speak out against him. If it was not for Fox News we would not know what the White House was doing to change America. They would already have the public option in place. The American people wouldn't have a clue about it. There would also be more national debts. They had control of the House of Representatives and the Senate and could have done what ever they wanted.

Thank God for Fox News and a few good Democrats that wouldn't give in to this idiot. We probably would be all socialist by now.

It is going to be interesting to see how many in Obama's circle of Democrats jump ship after the election if not before. It looks like Obama's free spending ways and vacations are coming to an abrupt end.

There was an interesting article that in essence states that Democrats are distancing themselves from the President and are not bragging about the misnomer health care and financial reform. They are also not mentioning the burgeoning debt that this Congress has created. So what does that leave them to talk about? I would say not much other than distorting the fact that since 2008 they have had super majorities in both houses of Congress and still can't get bills passed and then have the audacity to blame the opposition. Call them the party of "No" when in reality it is the Democrats that are the party of "No" for refusing to foster economic growth through reasonable taxation and responsible, enforced regulation. Because of their actions we now have an unemployment rate at 9.6%, officially, and unofficially at 15% to 20% in reality. The "hope" is that the American people will elect legislators that are in touch with their constituents and vote for measures that the majority of Americans want without the conniving backroom deals that have prevailed in this administration, which would be a real and hoped for refreshing "change" in Washington.

Have you noticed these incumbents are not in the least concerned for our country, or for hardworking taxpaying citizens all they care about is if they get reelected? These are the same scoundrels that jammed Obama care down our throats they did not give a dam about us then and they sure don't now. Does not matter if you are a Democrat, Independent or a Republican if you vote any of these rogues back into office they will do it again but this time they will not be concerned about being reelected so God help us. They will sell us down the river and Obama will be able to complete the destruction of our capitalistic system and initiate his Marxist government and peruse inserting Sharia law into our country. If that is what you want then by all means vote the Democrats that seem to all play follow the leader without and concern for their constituents.

You would think they would be bragging about their historic healthcare legislation.....you know, the one they didn't read that is so wonderful for all of us. Wasn't it Pelosi that stated "We need to pass this bill so that we can find out what is in it" or they could boast about their historic financial reform bill or their historic stimulus or their historic bailouts or their historic spending spree that has added dramatically to our national debt.....hmmm....guess we'll just resort to demonizing the opponent and avoid discussing the issues and their solutions.

The Associated Press tries to support the Democrats wherever possible, including straight forward lying. Their position in discussion is not about tax cuts for the riches. If a CEO earns some millions a year from a capital company, he is rich. A company owner earns $250,000 before taxes and reinvesting $150,000 after taxes to hold his company in the market maintaining jobs or creating more is not rich. Still, the mass of those hurt by Obama are not CEOs of big companies, they are entrepreneurs with small companies creating 80% of the jobs. So, obviously, Obama thinks, it's time to kill them.

Every scumbag who jumped up to applaud Calderon as he berated our people should be run out of Washington on a rail. These are professional politicians at their finest.

We need representatives that love America. Term limits should be implemented.

Think before voting. Don't vote Democrat. Don't vote Republican. Vote for the person who supported your view, regardless of party affiliation. That is the only way to hold these people accountable for their votes in the House of Representatives or the Senate. If you are for amnesty for illegals, then vote for the representative that voted for amnesty. If you are against amnesty, then vote for the person who voted against amnesty. Don't let lousy politicians that do not support your views mince words and then hide behind party labels. Know what you're representative's positions are before you vote for them.

Has anyone wondered how many of these politicians could hold a job in the private sector? Most would be fired, fined, or jailed for theft, fraud, or incompetence. There's more money to be made by most of these incompetents in the government than in the private world. Why is their pension after only two terms, equal to their full salary, paid with our dollars?

When are the Democrats going to understand that it is about the economy? Real disposable income, the money you and your family actually have for spending has remained stagnant since the Democrats and Obama took over in January 2009. In Harry Reid's home state of Nevada, real disposable income has plummeted under his leadership and Nevadans are poorer today than when Bush was president...good job, Harry and your Democrats....poverty has increased from 13% to 15% under this administration...the budget deficit is 1.5 trillion... the national debt is 14 trillion...unemployment is 15% nationwide, including those people Obama lists as chronically unemployed... (Just like his illegal alien aunt).

This is politics at its best. Treat the electorate with kid gloves and coddle them until the election is over than slam through the unpopular spending and pork barrel programs the politicians so love. Organized labor and tax takers will stand to gain a great deal if it works. The rest of us will just keep paying.

You will now see the Democrats throwing Obama, Pelosi and Reid, under the bus in the hopes that they can fool us into thinking that their votes were just mistakes for the pork stimulus, health care cram down, neither of bills that they even read.

Not one high level economist in our government has ever actually produced a product in this country. Look into all of them it's scary how predictable their background will be. How can these people be so arrogant? They are actually assuming they are capable of efficiently managing hundreds of millions of people directly and most of the world indirectly. Why are so many people in our country willing to give so much power to people who have nothing to show for their lives work but thousands of indoctrinated young minds?

GOD BLESS AMERICA

Thomas R. Meinders

CHAPTER THIRTY TWO

The National Anthem

We will try to address some of our concerns about the direction the United States has gone with regard to the playing of the National Anthem, saying the Pledge of Allegiance to the Flag, the use of the English language and the printing of government forms in Spanish. These areas are problems that are having a major effect on the direction that the United States of America has taken.

We are sure that this will anger all the non-English speaking people that are living in the United States of America. The human rights groups will be saying we are un-American. Good, then maybe we can get some action to correct these problems.

We find it disgraceful that we have to press 1 to talk to some businesses and/or the local, state and federal governments. Eliminate that press 2 for Spanish. If the American citizens want to do business in the United States then they should learn the English language. Is that really to much to ask? Anyone that thinks we are being unfair should try going to some other country and see if they will speak a special language for them. It will not happen.

The American Flag should be flown at every event that the public attends. Then the National Anthem should be played prior to the start of the event. All the people in attendance should be standing facing the Flag with their right hand over their heart and singing along. The National Anthem should be played at every assembly of every school in America and all the children should learn the words. It is a shame that the majority of Americans do not know the words. Everyday, the schools should say the Pledge of Allegiance to the Flag. Again, this will teach all the children the words. It also will instill the beliefs that our Country and Flag are worth protecting and understanding.

Printing our ballots to vote and the government forms in the United States in Spanish is an absolute disgrace and should be abolished. We find it disgusting that we need to pamper people that can not read English. If they can not read, how are they going to understand what they are voting for? It leads to votes that could have been swayed by organizations like ACORN.

These are things that most of the citizens were raised to believe in. It has just been the past several years that we have given up our principles. It is past time that we reinstate these policies.

It is too bad that the liberal media won't report such despicable events as this. If these Mexicans are so proud of their home country of Mexico, I suggest we ship them all back to Mexico. Instead of complaining about the new law recently passed in Arizona they simply enforces sound policy in a state is flooded with illegals, why don't we hear from the people with regard to the situation described below? It appears that they already finished their English homework. At the Montebello High School in California the Mexican students decided that the Mexican flag was more important then the American flag. This is the kind of stunts that you will not see reported in the mainstream media for fear of offending the Mexican population.

The protestors at the Montebello High School took the American flag off the school's flag pole and hung it upside down while putting up the Mexican flag over it. There were photos of this and were despicable.

This stunt may be the nail in the coffin of any guest worker or amnesty on the table in Washington. The image of the American subsumed to another and turned upside down on American soil is already spreading on the Internet forums and via e-mail.

If you choose to remain uninvolved, do not be amazed when you no longer have a nation to call our own nor anything you have worked for left, because it will have been 'redistributed' to the activists, while you choose the path of peace and stay out of the 'fray'. Check history, it is full of nations/empires that disappeared when its citizens no longer held on to their core beliefs and values. One person can make a difference. Just take the time to protect our country and be concerned. The battle for our secure borders and immigration laws that actually mean something, however, hasn't even begun.

I hope that this makes you as made as it makes me. If it doesn't it should matter to everyone in America that loves and protects their country.

We really need to protect our American children from this type of activity and only teach in English and with respect for our core principals such as the American flag and the National Anthem along with the Pledge of Allegiance.

For those who can not remember the words to the Pledge of Allegiance they are as follows:

I pledge Allegiance to the flag of the United States of America and to the Republic for which it stands, one nation under God, indivisible, with Liberty and Justice for all.

For those who can not remember the words to the National Anthem they are as follows:

The Star Spangled Banner

In 1814, Francis Scott Key wrote the poem, *Defense of Fort McHenry*. The poem was later put to the tune of (John Stafford Smith's song) *The Anacreontic Song*, modified somewhat, and retitled *The Star Spangled Banner*. Congress proclaimed *The Star Spangled Banner* the U.S. National Anthem in 1931.

Oh, say, can you see, by the dawn's early light,

What so proudly we hail'd at the twilight's last gleaming?

Whose broad stripes and bright stars, thro' the perilous fight,

O'er the ramparts we watch'd, were so gallantly streaming?

And the rockets' red glare, the bombs bursting in air,

Gave proof thro' the night that our flag was still there.

O say, does that star-spangled banner yet wave

O'er the land of the free and the home of the brave?

On the shore dimly seen thro' the mists of the deep,

Where the foe's haughty host in dread silence reposes,

What is that which the breeze, o'er the towering steep,

As it fitfully blows, half conceals, half discloses?

Now it catches the gleam of the morning's first beam,

In full glory reflected, now shines on the stream:

'Tis the star-spangled banner: O, long may it wave

O'er the land of the free and the home of the brave!

And where is that band who so vauntingly swore

That the havoc of war and the battle's confusion

A home and a country should leave us no more?

Their blood has wash'd out their foul footsteps' pollution.

No refuge could save the hireling and slave

From the terror of flight or the gloom of the grave:

And the star-spangled banner in triumph doth wave

O'er the land of the free and the home of the brave.

O, thus be it ever when freemen shall stand,

Between their lov'd homes and the war's desolation;

Blest with vict'ry and peace, may the heav'n-rescued land

Praise the Pow'r that hath made and preserv'd us a nation!

Then conquer we must, when our cause is just,

And this be our motto: "In God is our trust"

And the star-spangled banner in triumph shall wave

O'er the land of the free and the home of the brave!

The next time America the Beautiful is played at a sporting event or whatever sing along like a very proud American. For those who can not remember the words to America the Beautiful they are as follows:

America the Beautiful

Words by Katharine Lee Bates, Melody by Samuel Ward

O beautiful for spacious skies,

For amber waves of grain,

For purple mountain majesties

Above the fruited plain!

America! America!

God shed his grace on thee

And crown thy good with brotherhood

From sea to shining sea!

O beautiful for pilgrim feet

Whose stern impassioned stress

A thoroughfare of freedom beat

Across the wilderness!

America! America!

God mend thine every flaw,

Confirm thy soul in self-control,

Thy liberty in law!

O beautiful for heroes proved

In liberating strife.

Who more than self their country loved

And mercy more than life!

America! America!

May God thy gold refine

Till all success be nobleness

And every gain divine!

O beautiful for patriot dream

That sees beyond the years

Thine alabaster cities gleam

Undimmed by human tears!

America! America!

God shed his grace on thee

And crown thy good with brotherhood

From sea to shining sea!

O beautiful for halcyon skies,

For amber waves of grain,

For purple mountain majesties

Above the enameled plain!

America! America!

God shed his grace on thee

Till souls wax fair as earth and air

And music-hearted sea!

O beautiful for pilgrims feet,

Whose stem impassioned stress

A thoroughfare for freedom beat

Across the wilderness!

America! America!

God shed his grace on thee

Till paths be wrought through

wilds of thought

By pilgrim foot and knee!

O beautiful for glory-tale

Of liberating strife

When once and twice,

for man's avail

Men lavished precious life!

America! America!

God shed his grace on thee

Till selfish gain no longer stain

The banner of the free!

O beautiful for patriot dream

That sees beyond the years

Thine alabaster cities gleam

Undimmed by human tears!

America! America!

God shed his grace on thee

Till nobler men keep once again

Thy whiter jubilee!

Every American should be proud and display their respect to the United States. We are the greatest country in the world and we do not need to bow down to anyone. We are the home of the brave and proud to be free.

CHAPTER THIRTY THREE

Building a Mosque at Ground Zero

The only opinion that I have on building the mosque in the location they are planning is that the project looks like an attempt to glorify and celebrate the bombing of the World Trade Center.

I remember the events of 9/11/01 as clearly as they were yesterday. I can still see the first plane slamming into the initial tower and then while I was watching the building start to burn the second plane slammed into the other tower. It was just horrible watching as the buildings were burning and starting to collapse. There were people jumping out of windows to their death instead of burning. There were thousands of people running in the streets screaming while fearing for their life.

I know it is just my opinion, but the mosque should not be built on the proposed site. It is disgraceful to the American people.

We also need to remember that the Pentagon was also attacked and that an airplane was destroyed in Pennsylvania on the same morning. As much as the Muslims try to deny it, the fact remains they are trying to build this mosque to celebrate their victory in the United States of America.

Why doesn't public opinion count?

This is not about religion, it is about respect. Why would anyone support a project like this while the vast majority of the Americans do not want it built at ground zero and it is being built as a monument to the destruction of the World Trade Center?

Do Islamic Center developers have the funds to build?

The Mosque is nothing more than an in your face victory building. We are paying (our tax money) for a Muslim that dislikes America to go on a fund raising trip to the Middle East. Talk about rubbing our faces in the ashes of the World Trade Center. Come on people wake up. Why don't they build it some where else? Ground zero is where they had a great victory over the United States of America.

Here's the main issue. When one looks at the life of the founder of Islam we see a conqueror and a warrior. Members of any religion look to their founder and try to follow their example. That is what has non Muslims concerned. Anybody that thinks they are making God happy by wearing a beard or other "special clothing" is living in a fantasy world. If you look at a map of the world and color the countries based on religious beliefs you will notice that predominately Muslims countries do not allow the same freedoms that we have and that we want to keep.

Even if the funds are not raised to build this mosque, it can hardly be said that this has been much ado about nothing. The core issue here is not one of religious freedoms or tolerance vs. intolerance. There are already more than 100 mosques in NYC alone so how can anyone say this is an issue of religious intolerance? The core issue is Imam Rauf's continued provocation of the American people...implying that America was complicit in the murders of 9/11 because of our world view. The hypocrisy is rampant in this whole issue...the left wingers proclaim the Constitutional separation of church and state while funding $16,000 to the Imam to travel to the middle east to solicit funds for the building of this mosque. Obama proclaims during a Ramadan celebration dinner that building the mosque near the graveyard of 3000 innocent victims is the "right of the Muslim people", while out of the other side of his mouth proclaiming himself a

Christian The Imam and his followers are eager to put "conquered" to the site of this proposed mosque, just as the Moors did in Cordoba, Spain.

This is not a religion. It is an organization that promotes murder/terrorism (i.e. kill the infidels those that are not Muslim/the majority of Americans). It promotes slavery of a whole gender. It promotes rape/assault on little children in the name of marriage. Mr. President and Congress bring our troops home and fight the terrorist that are here on America soil. When you fail to enact laws that severely punish criminals that commit murder and rape the only thing that makes sense to me is that you are one of them or would like to be. I think more women need to run for office and also register to vote, and then just do it.

The American citizens are not telling Muslims they can't worship, we are simply asking them to consider the sensitivity of the situation. Honestly, if the Muslims are trying to restore their image after the 9/11 attacks; then it's pretty simple don't build this mosque near ground zero. The building of this mosque would be no different if the Japanese decided to erect a Buddhist shrine near Pearl Harbor. But, at least the Japanese have the common courtesy and respect of our fallen dead from the actions of their extremists. Build the mosque somewhere else.

Just as Muslim customs should be respected in the Middle East, why don't they respect the customs and traditions of lands they live in? Instead they want to use sharia law and not assimilate with the host nation's people. Yes, there are Muslims that do, but many do not. Those that don't want the host country to change to the Muslim way.

Muslims tend to destroy instead of create. Look at the daily headlines of hate and violence. Are Christians and Jews perfect? Nobody is. But Christians and Jews have created products and methods to help mankind and animals. Christians and Jews have made life easier and more productive through inventions.

The Muslims have lost trust and respect around the world thanks to their violence and hatred that we see on a daily basis in the news. Yes, there are good Muslims who want peace. Sadly they are lumped together with the radicals. How many Muslims have denounced worldwide attacks? How many have danced in the streets as they watched the World Trade Center crumble?

Don't give us this crap about being a racist or bigot? The racists and bigots are the Muslims. I understand Muslims in Saudi Arabia will not allow churches to be built? Democracy and religious freedom dies when Islam rules. Those are perhaps the biggest reasons we are against Islam. We want religious and other freedoms in America. Look at history.

Let's face it, the Muslims want to sit and pray somewhere where they can overlook their greatest accomplishment against the rest of us "infidels." The Koran preaches hate against all non-Muslims.

Truthfully they do not have the right to build a mosques or anything else in the United States. Freedom of religion does not give any group the right to build a building of any kind. Can't you worship God without a church? Does your faith only work when you are at church or does it work all the time. No where in the constitution does it say you have the right to build a building to worship in but just simply you have the right to worship. Even if you have the freedom of religion it doesn't mean you can practice it. Some religions say you can have more than one wife but here in the United States. That isn't legal so you can only have one. Islamization occurs when there are sufficient Muslims in a country to agitate for their so-called 'religious rights.' When politically correct and culturally diverse societies agree to 'the reasonable' Muslim demands for their 'religious rights,' they also get the other components under the table. Here's how it works (percentages source CIA: The World Fact Book (2007)). As long as the Muslim population remains around 1% of any given country they will be regarded as a peace-loving minority and not as a threat to anyone. In fact, they may be featured in articles and films, stereotyped for their colorful uniqueness:

United States — Muslim 1.0%

Australia — Muslim 1.5%

Canada — Muslim 1.9%

China — Muslim 1%-2%

Italy — Muslim 1.5%

Norway — Muslim 1.8%

At 2% and 3% they begin to proselytize from other ethnic minorities and disaffected groups with major recruiting from the jails and among street gangs:

Denmark — Muslim 2%

Germany — Muslim 3.7%

United Kingdom — Muslim 2.7%

Spain — Muslim 4%

Thailand — Muslim 4.6%

From 5% on they exercise an inordinate influence in proportion to their percentage of the population. They will push for the introduction of halal (clean by Islamic standards) food, thereby securing food preparation jobs for Muslims. They will increase pressure on supermarket chains to feature it on their shelves — along with threats for failure to comply.

France — Muslim 8%

Philippines — Muslim 5%

Sweden — Muslim 5%

Switzerland — Muslim 4.3%

The Netherlands — Muslim 5.5%

Trinidad &Tobago — Muslim 5.8%

At this point, they will work to get the ruling government to allow them to rule themselves under Sharia, the Islamic Law. The ultimate goal of Islam is to convert the world & to establish Sharia law over the entire world.

When Muslims reach 10% of the population, they will increase lawlessness as a means of complaint about their conditions (Paris –car-burnings). Any non-Muslim action that offends Islam will result in uprisings and threats (Amsterdam – Mohammed cartoons).

Guyana — Muslim 10%

India — Muslim 13.4%

Israel — Muslim 16%

Kenya — Muslim 10%

Russia — Muslim 10-15%

After reaching 20% expect hair-trigger rioting, jihad militia formations, sporadic killings and church and synagogue burning:

Ethiopia — Muslim 32.8%

At 40% you will find widespread massacres, chronic terror attacks and ongoing militia warfare:

Bosnia — Muslim 40%

Chad — Muslim 53.1%

Lebanon — Muslim 59.7%

From 60% you may expect unfettered persecution of non-believers and other religions, sporadic ethnic cleansing (genocide), use of Sharia Law as a weapon and Jizya, the tax placed on infidels:

Albania — Muslim 70%

Malaysia — Muslim 60.4%

Qatar — Muslim 77.5%

Sudan — Muslim 70%

After 80% expect State run ethnic cleansing and genocide:

Bangladesh — Muslim 83%

Egypt — Muslim 90%

Gaza — Muslim 98.7%

Indonesia — Muslim 86.1%

Iran — Muslim 98%

Iraq — Muslim 97%

Jordan — Muslim 92%

Morocco — Muslim 98.7%

Pakistan — Muslim 97%

Palestine — Muslim 99%

Syria — Muslim 90%

Tajikistan — Muslim 90%

Turkey — Muslim 99.8%

United Arab Emirates — Muslim 96%

100% will usher in the peace of 'Dar-es-Salaam' — the Islamic House of Peace — there's supposed to be peace because everybody is a Muslim: we know however that this isn't true is it?

Afghanistan — Muslim 100%

This needs to be the only flag at ground zero

GOD BLESS AMERICA

CHAPTER THIRTY FOUR

The Summary

We admit that we have taken a simple approach to the problems that we are facing in the United States. That is something that the federal government does not understand. Every piece of legislation that is proposed has to be very complex and drawn out. That way the Congress can attach pork bills to the bill. There should be legislation that does not allow any pork added to any bill. If the bill that is presented to the Congress for a vote can not stand up on its own merit then the bill should not be passed. No exceptions. This will put an end to excessive spending for local projects as a way of saying thank you for supporting my legislation. We need truth in legislation and total transparency. Let the people have a right to read the bill and make sure every member of both houses has read legislation prior to taking a vote and having it signed into law.

The problems that we are facing in the recovery of the United States are not going to be simple. However, they must be done or we will no longer by the best country in the world to live in and our standard of living is deteriorating at a very rapid pace. We are going to be faced by hostile complaints from all the special interest groups that always put their interest first instead of the best interest of the entire United States.

Let's not forget the real reason why "immigrant rights" groups went apoplectic about SB-1070 - because for the first time ever it would take away the free pass illegals have in the United States once they get past the border. When state and local police across the United States are allowed to check their status when they get pulled over, you can wave by to your new neighbors who are illegals.

The US Constitution is a fluid document that is interpreted in light of prevailing customs and norms. 200+ years ago, what might have been acceptable criminal punishment is now deemed cruel and inhumane. Similarly, 200+ years ago, or indeed up until the 1920s, virtually anyone could immigrate to the United States. The times have changed and we have strong laws on our books. When the federal government chooses not to enforce each and every law for one group of people but not others, and that has an adverse impact on United States citizens' property and safety, states should be able to craft supplemental but non-conflicting legislation to protect its citizens. In every poll out there on the Arizona law, a minimum of 66% of United States citizens agree. This is not a race issue. If there were 20 million illegal Europeans in the United States they would need to go as well.

There could be another blemish on the way the Obama administration has been operating since he took office.

According to sources that watch the inner workings of the federal government, a smack down of Barack 0bama by the U.S. Supreme Court may be inevitable.

Ever since 0bama assumed the office of President, critics have hammered him on a number of Constitutional issues. Critics have complained that much if not all of 0bama's major initiatives run headlong into Constitutional roadblocks on the power of the federal government.

0bama certainly did not help himself in the eyes of the Court when he used the venue of the State of the Union address early in the year to publicly flog the Court over its ruling that the First Amendment grants the right to various organizations to run political ads during the time of an election.

The tongue lashing clearly did not sit well with the Court, as was demonstrated by Justice Sam Alito, who publicly shook his head and stated under his breath, 'That's not true,' when Obama told a flat-out lie concerning the Court's ruling.

As it has turned out, this was a watershed moment in the relationships between the executive and the judicial branches of the federal government. Obama publicly declared war on the court, even as he blatantly continued to propose legislation that flies in the face of every known Constitutional principle upon which this nation has stood for over 200 years.

Obama has even identified Chief Justice John Roberts as his number one enemy, that is, apart from Fox News and Rush Limbaugh. And it is no accident that the one swing vote on the court, Justice Anthony Kennedy, stated recently that he has no intention of retiring until Obama is gone.

Apparently, the Court has had enough. The Roberts Court has signaled, in a very subtle manner, of course, that it intends to address the issues about which Obama critics have been screaming to high heaven. A ruling against Obama on any one of these important issues could potentially cripple the Administration.

Such a thing would be long overdue. First, there is Obama Care, which violates the Constitutional principle barring the federal government from forcing citizens to purchase something. And no, this is not the same thing as states requiring drivers to purchase car insurance, as some of the intellectually impaired claim.

The Constitution limits the federal government, not the individual state governments, from such things, and further, not everyone has to drive, and thus, a citizen could opt not to purchase car insurance by simply deciding not to drive a vehicle. In the Obama Care world, however, no citizen can opt out of coverage.

Second, sources state that the Roberts court has quietly accepted information concerning discrepancies in Obama's history that raise serious questions about his eligibility for the office of President. The charge goes far beyond the birth certificate issue. This information involves possible fraudulent use of a Social Security number in Connecticut, while Obama was a high school student in Hawaii. And that is only the tip of the iceberg.

Third, several cases involving possible criminal activity, conflicts of interest, and pay-for-play cronyism could potentially land many Administration officials, if not the President himself, in hot water with the Court. Frankly, in the years this writer has observed politics, nothing comes close to comparing with the rampant corruption of this Administration, not even during the Nixon years. Nixon and the Watergate conspirators look like choirboys compared to the jokers that populate this Administration.

In addition, the Court will eventually be forced to rule on the dreadful decision of the 0bama Department of Justice to sue the state of Arizona. That too, could send the 0bama doctrine of open borders to an early grave, given that the Administration refuses to enforce federal law on illegal aliens.

And finally, the biggie that could potentially send the entire house of cards tumbling in a free-fall is the latest revelation concerning the 0bama Holder Department of Justice and its refusal to pursue the New Black Panther Party. The group is caught on tape committing felonies by attempting to intimidate Caucasian voters into staying away from the polls.

A whistle-blower who resigned from the Department of Justice is now charging Holder with the deliberate refusal to pursue cases against Blacks, particularly those who are involved in radical hate-groups, such as the New Black Panthers, who have been caught on tape calling for the murder of white people and their babies.

This one is a real biggie that could send the entire Administration crumbling. That is, if the Justices have the guts to draw a line in the quick sand at the Constitution and the Bill of Rights.

"Some people spend an entire lifetime wondering if they made a difference in the world. But the United States Armed Forces don't have that problem." .... Ronald Reagan

The Governor of Arizona is correct in protecting Arizona residents and borders. Many people realize now that these illegals have a mission. Populate the United States and then spread like roaches because they think they have a right to come and take and demand we take care of their families and offspring. The idiots that have refused to enforce our laws are at fault and should be deported themselves.

Americans are Americans and we used to stand for values and principles that were irrefutable. Values that allowed us to look for a job and now the liberals and dummies want equality for these illegals.

I hope this law is allowed to go through, because if it doesn't I believe we will have another 10 million illegal immigrants in this country also demanding "their rights". It is shameful to think that even our own government is bringing suit against the citizens of America who want control and enforcement of our immigration laws. It boggles the mind to think this group who happens to be Hispanic, can break our laws by entering this country illegally steal social security cards because they "just want to work", receive free healthcare, have children who automatically become citizens, march on our streets with their country of origin flag demanding their rights and still expect to become citizens of this country with no consequence, which is exactly what will happen if this law is blocked. This country is going to become another third world country if we do not stop illegal immigration. These illegals have helped lower wages in this country and have taken jobs that Americans can and will do. Illegals do not and should not have the support of our government to circumvent our laws. It is a disgrace and an insult to the American people.

We are going to take a look at the suggestions that we made and how they would affect the deficit of the United States.

First, if the proposals outlined were implemented we would have a reduction in the deficit of $130,068 billion per year from discretionary spending of the government alone. Nice start isn't it?

We discussed repealing some of the legislation that has been passed against the will of the people. By repealing the following three pieces of legislation we would be able to cut the deficit by a total of $567 billion from the 2011 federal deficit.

When will the President learn that we can not solve the country's problems by spending money that we do not have? It is so basic that even a cave man could figure it out.

Repeal the bill signed into law on September 26, 2010 President Obama signed into law H. R. 5297 the Small Business Bill. This bill authorizes $30 billion for new loans and $12 billion in tax relief programs for small businesses.

No one knows for sure what is in the H.R. 4872 bill or had an opportunity to find out before it was voted on and signed into law by Obama. This bill is expected to add over $900 billion to the deficit. We are predicting that in the initial year of the bill it is going to add $300 billion to the deficit this year.

Repeal the balance of the Stimulus Bill that has about $225 billion in funds that have not been allocated.

We also discussed the changes in the corporate income tax structure and how it affects our deficit. Just the change on taxing the excessive compensation that is paid to corporate executive with stock payments would reduce the deficit by generating $7.2 billion in income taxes from this one item. Increasing the corporate income tax rate from 35% to 40% would provide an additional $58.7 billion in tax revenues per year.

We discussed the President's Budget requests $19.6 billion for the Housing Choice Voucher program to help more than two million extremely low to low-income families with rental assistance to live in decent housing in neighborhoods of their choice. This looks like another welfare project to encourage the poor to vote. What people will wonder is just how many of these low income families are illegals?

I find it offensive that the President thinks that the low income families need to live in the neighborhoods of their choice. What about providing creative programs that will give them a chance to get out of the low income range? The building of the fence on the Mexican border would create thousands of jobs. There needs to be one situation on being hired and that would be that the workers must be legal American citizens.

Was everyone else aware of the fact that there was a Congressional Hispanic Caucus (CHC) and a Black Caucus? What happened to the White Caucus? It seems like there should be equal standing for all the members of Congress and not establishing segregation among the members. These members will probably by the first to play the race card on any legislation that they do not understand or want. The practice should be abolished in Congress.

The poor House Democrats are whining that these 23 CHC members are not paying their dues and that they are the stingiest when it comes to giving funds to the Democratic Party. Seems like they function the same at all levels and think that there might be a free lunch somewhere. I sure hope that someone has checked their immigration status to make sure that they are eligible to hold office. Does that remind you of someone else?

Some Hispanic lawmakers cited the challenging political and economic environment as the reason for their scant giving, while others said they are frustrated with the lack of progress on comprehensive immigration reform. Those Members said they don't want their campaign dollars funding Democrats who have blocked progress on an overhaul. This makes it very clear that these members are going to be trying to block any legislation that will prevent amnesty for the Mexican people. I wonder if any of these members of the CHC has ever read the Constitution of the United States. Possibly they need to understand that the laws of our country allow for legal immigration and part of that process is to study the English language and understand our laws. Legal immigrants also must wait 5 years before they can apply for citizenship and then must pass an entrance exam before being sworn in by a federal judge. When illegals are granted amnesty they will not stop coming and ruining our economy and life style. We can not have our country destroyed in this manner.

In November 2007 the CHC boycotted a procedural vote on a Democratic tax bill that was a high priority for leadership. The move prompted an angry exchange between the CHC who helped spearhead the boycott to protest Democratic support for a Republican English only proposal. CHC members were furious in 2005 when Democratic leaders urged vulnerable Frontline Democrats to vote for a GOP proposal designed to crack down on illegal immigrants. CHC Vice Chairman Charlie Gonzalez said he needs to worry about his own race this cycle.

Now we can start to understand why there has not been any legislation to curb the flow of illegals into the United States and we print our government forms in two languages. This is a disgrace to the citizens of the United

States and wastes millions of dollars every year. How can we continue to let our government act as they please instead of how the people want?

The American citizens are facing the reality that the CHC is going to promote the Democratic policies. They realize that heavy Democratic losses are going to impede the movement of the CHC priorities and in particular on immigration reform. The CHC is not going to be able to pass the sort of bills that many people in this Caucus would like to see passed if we have fewer members. In other words their dreams of amnesty will have a much harder time without the CHC. In looking at all the CHC rhetoric there doesn't seem be any platform about protecting the integrity and well being of all of the Americans.

Obama and friends in latest spin of the news

At a meeting of the President's Economic Recovery Advisory Board the following information was discussed and released in a press release by Daily Finance, an AOL Money and Finance Site.

The President's Economic Recovery Advisory Board was intending to discuss colleges and worker training. Instead President Obama got into a spirited debate with a business advisory group about whose tax cuts should be extended and for how long. Some of the people that were in attendance included Martin Feldstein, Harvard economist, William Donaldson, Chairman of the Securities and Exchange Commission, Paul Volcker Former Federal Reserve Chairman, and Penny Pritzker, a real estate executive and longtime Democratic fundraiser who serves on the board, said panel members were discussing whether they should take a formal position on the issue of extending the Bush Tax Cuts.

Everyone would agree that this was a meeting of some of the most intelligent individuals in the country. Right? Well, this is a direct quote from the article by Mark S. Smith of the Associated Press posted 4:18 PM 10/04/10.

When asked about extending the Bush Tax Cuts Obama replied that his stand would benefit 98 percent of American taxpayers. "You'd think (that) would provide some level of certainty," Obama also reiterated his view that top-income tax brackets would do little to boost the recovery, since the wealthy aren't holding off buying flat-screen TVs and other big-ticket purchases for lack of a tax cut. Plus, he said, those tax cuts are unaffordable.

"If we were going to spend $700 billion, it seems it would be wiser having that $700 billion going to folks who would spend that money right away," Obama said. What the President is not telling the people that this could be over a 10 year period. Quite an omission because it appears that he is insinuating it will happen this year. That is one terrific spin that is being put on the Americans by the mainstream media.

None of these high ranking intelligent individuals that attended this meeting were honest enough to point out that fact to the President. Let the world think he is protecting the taxpayers. This is to get more votes.

Obama dismissed the notion that the well-off — he included himself — would simply "take our ball and go home" if they didn't continue to get a big tax cut.

Former Federal Reserve Chairman Paul Volcker, who heads the advisory group, backed up Obama. "I want to assure you that my psychology will not be affected," he declared amid laughter.

What all of these individuals should be laughing at is their stupidity. Do some simple math. Obama has said we are going to spend $700 billion. The President also said that it was going to come from the 98 percent of the richest taxpayers. Let me get this straight. Previously the Bush Tax Cuts were going to cost the taxpayers about 3.7 trillion over ten years. That is putting quite a spin for the news media. It would amount to $70 billion per year. The facts are that the richest taxpayers are paying approximately 50% of the individual income taxes collected. The budget report shows that all individual taxpayers were projected to pay the government a total of $1.121 trillion for 2011. That would mean that the richest would be paying $560.5 billion of the income tax bill. If you increase the rate from 35% to 39.6% it is an increase of 11.61% to these individuals and not 4.6% as the President

is claiming. Even then the amount of additional income taxes the rich would pay would be $63 billion. Where is the additional $7 billion going to come from?

Then we have Congress debating whether to dole out another $700 billion in tax breaks for the wealthiest 2% of Americans. Instead of paying down the debt, creating jobs or investing in our education system, this money would simply line the pockets of a select few -- most of whom haven't asked for a tax cut and don't need it. When Congress starts to be concerned about the deficit they need to realize that it is the spending without any means of paying for it that creates the deficit.

The President is slamming the Republicans for spending cut plans. That is really lame since the spending bills have been forced through both houses that are for Democratic spending. Does anyone else see through this scam?

Page 37 of the President's proposed 2011 budget.

Laying a new foundation for economic growth and prosperity for working families will take a change in policies and programs to unleash the creativity and hard work of the American people. But to prevent our country from backsliding into the irresponsibility of the past, we need to change how Washington works. We have seen the consequences of fiscal recklessness, of tolerance for programs that no longer work or are outdated, and of a government that is most open to those with access and influence. The deficits, wasted resources, and special treatment squandered funds that could have been used to help Americans gain or retain a foothold in the middle class and enjoy what every family wants: a good job, a roof over their heads, excellent schools for their children, affordable and high-quality health care, and a secure retirement.

The President never ceases to try and convince the taxpayers how great he is and that he will be our savior. What a crock of the remains left by the south end of a donkey heading north. Does the President really think anyone is going to believe any of this?

Looking at the details of the Presidents proposed budget for 2011 on page

151 it shows that revenue from individual income taxes for the year ending on September 30, 2011 will be $1.121 trillion.

The following newsletter has been included. I write these on a continuing basis to try and keep the taxpayers informed about some of the problems we are having with the economy and other problems in America.

"MY AMERICAN DREAM"

Newsletter   **October 6, 2010**

Volume 2010-31   **www.my-american-dream.org**

We are going to try and figure out whether the rich are providing their share of the tax burden to the United States of America. We hear so much about how the ultra rich are going to donate 50% of their wealth to charity. What about paying some income or gift or estate tax to the federal government?

For the sake of not offending any of the extremely wealthy we will use Waldo Freeloader as the rich citizen. Waldo Freeloader accumulated the bulk of his $5 billion in wealth from starting a company in America. He received 50 million shares when American Dream, Inc. was founded in 2005. When Waldo founded the Company he had invested a total of $25,000. After creating a great product that was highly successful the American Dream, Inc. decided to take the company public. The offering was a huge success and the Company raised $20 million. The public received 10 million shares at $2.00 per share. Waldo still owned the majority of the company. Waldo still controlled 83.33% of the Company after the public offering was completed.

After several huge successes the price of the Company's shares went to $100 per share. Now Waldo has had the value of his shares increase to $5 billion. Since the price was now to expensive for most investors the Company decides to do a stock split to lower the price to $20.00 per share. This will require a 5 for 1 split. Now Waldo has hit the jackpot. He now has a total of 250 million shares with a value of his stock in American Dream, Inc. is not worth $5 billion. It is time to be grateful and start giving it to charity.

During the years that American Dream, Inc. was creating this huge amount of wealth Waldo was living the good life from his earnings as the Chief Executive of the Company. Waldo has not had to sell any of his shares.

It would be nice to know just how much gift taxes are going to be paid by Waldo when he gives the wealth to charity. We are going to assume that the gifts to charity are in the form of stock in American Dream, Inc. If Waldo was required to sell the shares and then donate the proceeds it would create income taxes on the sale and the gift. So it is pretty obvious that the gift would be in stock. What Waldo is doing is evading the tax on the gain of his stock and paying the income tax on the gain. Yes, it is very smart on Waldo's part but not in the best interest of the taxpayers.

What we need to do is make sure that Waldo has filed the proper gift tax forms and paid the taxes so that the government receives some of his charity.

Possibly a new piece of legislation should be enacted to change the charitable laws to only allow the gift of cash or property other than stock in publicly traded companies. This would require the sale of the shares before the contribution could be made and therefore the income taxes on the huge gains that taxpayers like Waldo would have to pay. You can hear the screams of the rich already. The charitable organizations will be screaming that they are not receiving their fair share because the donations would be lower.

We also need to consider whether the charitable contribution remains in the United States. We agree that it is great to address world problems but we have way too many serious problems in the United States. Another thing we need to make sure of is that until the law is changed we need to make sure that if a contribution is made with stock that it is valued at the current market price and not what Waldo paid for it. The gift tax rate tops out at 35% for anything over $500,000. If a gift of 1 million shares of American Dream, Inc. stock was made with the current market value of $20.00 the gift would be worth $20 million. If the cost was used as a basis the gift would have been $500.00. The cost to the taxpayers of the United States would be $7 million.

LAST MINUTE ADDITION

After reading parts of the H.R. 4321 bill that has been presented for vote or passed. This bill needs to re repealed or amended in such a manner that there are no provisions for back door amnesty. This bill contains almost the same language as the bill Harry Reid tried to attach for providing amnesty for college and military service.

Repealing 'Obamacare' Will Define Republicans in 2011

WASHINGTON (Dec. 11) -- Forget tax cuts, gays in the military and even immigration. In 2011, *the* hot-button issue for newly ascendant Republicans will be the health care law.

For those who thought "death panels" were so '09, or that President Barack Obama settled the matter when he signed the overhaul into law, think again. If there is one issue that promises to unite Republicans everywhere, it's the federal Patient Protection and Affordable Care Act. Consider.

The next speaker of the House, John Boehner, has pledged to repeal and replace what Republicans derisively call "Obamacare."

House Minority Leader John Boehner of Ohio stands behind a copy of the Democrats' version of the health care bill during a news conference on Capitol Hill in Washington on Oct. 29, 2009. On December 13, 2010 a Federal Judge ruled that the Obamacare law was unconstitutional.

Sarah Palin, when asked by Time magazine what she would do if elected president in 2012, said "the first priority 'of the next Republican president' should be 'to sign a bill for the repeal and replacement of Obamacare with true free-market, patient-centered reform.' "

Republican governors, from Minnesota presidential hopeful Tim Pawlenty to Rick Perry in Texas, to those who haven't even taken office yet, such as Wisconsin's Scott Walker, have balked at implementing the health care law in their states.

GOP legislators in 40 states have introduced bills to block all or part of the law.

State attorneys general, most of them Republicans, have gone to court to challenge the constitutionality of the law's "individual mandate," which in order to create a large enough risk pool for insurers requires most Americans to have coverage or pay a penalty.

A sign of just how polarizing the health care debate has become: Four of the five federal judges who have weighed in so far have decided along party lines, with two Clinton appointees upholding the law and judges appointed by Ronald Reagan and George W. Bush allowing challenges to proceed. On Wednesday, another Bush appointee, U.S. District Judge Susan Wigenton, broke party ranks when she dismissed a lawsuit in New Jersey.

The law is likely to end up at the U.S. Supreme Court. Until then, critics say the court of public opinion gives them a potent political issue.

"Obamacare is the biggest example of government overreach we've ever seen," said Mike Connolly of the fiscally conservative Club for Growth. "It is the single greatest threat to economic freedom and growth, so it will remain a huge and defining issue for the 2012 campaign."

Tom Borelli of the National Center for Public Policy Research, a conservative think tank here, said there is "tremendous momentum" among the voters behind GOP gains: "Rolling back Obamacare is the top priority for tea party activists."

Frank Luntz, the GOP message guru who counseled Fox News commentators to always talk about "government-run" health care, said as the presidential primary takes over the national political debate, Republican lawmakers "will be driven to undermine Obamacare in every way possible. GOP primary voters want nothing short of repeal and they don't want compromise."

Risks and Rewards

But if Republicans focus on "Obamacare," will they make the same strategic mistake Democrats were accused of in the last election -- namely, putting the issue of health care over jobs and the economy? Despite passage of the historic legislation, voters did not give Democrats the credit some thought they deserved.

Yet as the law gradually takes effect, the potential for political rewards and risks will certainly rise.

"It is absolutely going to heat up and be a hot topic through 2014," when most provisions will be implemented, said Erikka Knuti of the Health Information Campaign, a consumer education group that supports the law. "If they [Republicans] make repeal of health care their central platform, they're leaving themselves up for big problems and backlash. Nobody's going to want to go back to being denied coverage for a pre-existing condition."

Yet that is exactly where many new members of Congress want to go. North Carolina's Renee Ellmers, a Palin protégé opposes requiring insurers to accept patients with pre-existing conditions -- including pregnancy. Austin Scott of Georgia, another House freshman, was asked if there was any part of the law he supported. He replied, "No, ma'am, there are not."

Ideologically tough attitudes like those have raised questions about whether Boehner will be able to control the "Tea Party Congress" or if new members will adjust their thinking to congressional reality.

If polls are to be believed, both may have to reconsider their positions.

While a slight majority opposes the health care law, there is evidence that many people like individual provisions such as allowing children up to age 26 to stay on their parents' insurance. The latest Kaiser health tracking poll revealed just a quarter want all or part of the law repealed.

Repeal or Repeal and Replace?

Republicans have adjusted their slogan from "repeal" to "repeal and replace." Yet even that will be difficult. They may have new power in the House and more seats in the Senate, but Republicans still lack enough votes to overcome a filibuster or override a presidential veto.

House Republicans will, however, be able to highlight the 906-page law's costs and uncertainties in oversight hearings that could "convince people that the plan is an administrative nightmare," said John Pitney, a former GOP Hill staffer who teaches at Claremont McKenna College in California. "The risk for Republicans is that they might botch the 'replace' part of the 'repeal and replace' approach."

Even before the 112th Congress convenes, Republicans can claim at least a small victory, though. The Obama administration has retreated on a tax reporting requirement that businesses found onerous.

But on the big things like health insurance exchanges and the individual mandate, Democrats are unlikely to budge. They'll get help from liberal groups that are painting GOP lawmakers as "health care hypocrites" who accept federally subsidized coverage but oppose it for 32 million uninsured Americans.

Luntz says Republicans must tread carefully not to alienate independents and centrists who may not like much of the health care law but do want changes made. "Republicans can't just call for the repeal of Obamacare," he said, "they need a clearly defined alternative."

But time, supporters say, is ultimately on their side.

"Benefits are beginning to play out," said Judy Feder, senior fellow at the liberal Center for American Progress. "The burden is on the opponents. They have a tough row to hoe to take back the House of Representatives.

What Americans think

If Americans took the time to find out who is responsible for the loss of jobs in America, maybe they would understand who is responsible. It was the

103rd Congress of 1993, controlled by the Democrats in both the House and Senate that approved WTO and NAFTA that allowed companies to move operations overseas for cheap labor and bring their products into America duty free. Bill Clinton was president and the Democrats were in control of Congress. Over the last 16 years most of the jobs in our country have been moved overseas. In 2006, the Democrats gained control of the Congress again. Most of us would love to turn back the clock for the last four years. Our economy has gone to hell since they took control of the Congress. Last year, Canada brought in over 3,000 producing new oil wells. We buy 30% of our oil from Canada. Why hasn't our country drilled any new wells? Are the oil wells in Canada wrecking their country? No, they are reducing their trade deficit while the trade deficit in the United States continues to grow.

The President got half the message of the 2010 election; he didn't get the part about deficit spending, though, and Pelosi and the rest of the New Party of No are trying to load tons of pork into the bill. Obama put icing on the cake when he called Clinton in to save the day. Is Bill Clinton the designated president when the going gets tough? Obama is an obscene joke.

Thanks for the Tea Party. We need to get rid of big Government starting with Obamacare. And bring back the private sector so everyone can have a job. Fifty percent of the people are supporting the other fifty percent right now, how long can that continue before the whole system collapses. We need jobs for everyone not more illegals to support. Not more entitlements for those unwillingly to work. Or jobs sent to third world countries. Here's a novel Idea, let's have all our company's relocate to America?

Ever go the Post Office, or maybe the Social Security office, or any government service for that matter? When you go to any of these places you see the future of your health care. The government employees having to take their breaks and a untrained employee there who decides what services you are qualified to receive. Again, try real hard and think of who is in these positions. The people who receive these services now are used to being slaves to the government and they don't know any better. Just wait until you have to stand in line behind the illegals with her 5 anchor babies and can't speak a word of English, while the woman who is sitting behind the desk tells her, Baby, you gotta sign dees papers befores you gets yo healfcare. While you have worked and have paid your $800.00 a month for the last 20 years, and the same obese employee tells you while you are waiting with your sick little boy or girl, Sir or Honey, you jus gonna have to wait like da rest of dees peoples.

Pride in America

All Americans can and should be proud of our Country.

HERE IS A LATE TIDBIT FOR EVERYONE

White House Friends Get Hundreds of ObamaCare Waivers

The White House has quietly granted more than 200 waivers for new healthcare act requirements, essentially granting repeal to more than a million people. For average Americans, however, only outright repeal through our campaign will bring relief from this destructive law.

Unions like the Service Employee's International Union (SEIU), perhaps the most partisan of all Mr. Obama's supporters (who devoted millions of dollars to attacking Republican candidates), was one of the first waivers granted -- allowing their members an "escape hatch"

from ObamaCare. All unions were granted exemption from income taxes on the value of high cost plans -- unlike every other American.

Adding salt to the wound, the law exempts the President, Vice-President, cabinet officers and Capitol Hill staffers who work for Congressional Committees, among others.

The promise repeated over and over again that average Americans could keep their health care coverage has now been admitted to be false with the Administration itself conceding that as many of eight out of ten existing programs will disappear under onerous new coverage requirements.

"PRIDE IN AMERICA"
I'm proud to be an American
I'm proud of the "Pledge of Allegiance"
I'm proud of the "National Anthem"
I'm proud to display the "American Flag"
I'm proud to defend the "American Freedoms"
I'm proud to communicate in "English"
I'm proud of freedom of "Religion"
I'm proud to be an American
God Bless the United States of America

Thomas R. Meinders

ABOUT THE AUTHOR

 I was born in Grundy Center, Iowa on October 21, 1937 and raised in Cedar Falls, Iowa until I enlisted in the United States Air Force. I have served my country for 8 years, 1 month and 6 days and have two honorable discharges to show for it. I am currently raising my 9 year old son as a single parent and living on social security. I have been in the stock brokerage business for about 20 years and an accountant for about 25 years. During the last 10 years I have attempted to help start-up companies to have a method of raising capital. As with all start-up companies some of them made it and the majority of them did not. That is just the nature of the start-up business. Through it all I have kept my sanity and have not lost my ability to think. I have been blessed with reasonable intelligence and have the ability to use common sense. I have also written "America Can Recover" "Bashing Sarah Palin" and "A Beautiful America"

www.ingramcontent.com/pod-product-compliance
Lightning Source LLC
Chambersburg PA
CBHW030259290526
45785CB00001B/141